JOHN GREGSON · DINAH SHERIDAN
IN
GENEVIEVE 'U'
COLOUR BY TECHNICOLOR
GFD

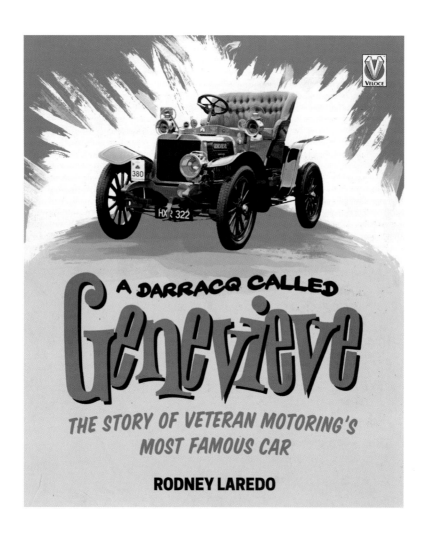

A DARRACQ CALLED

Genevieve

THE STORY OF VETERAN MOTORING'S MOST FAMOUS CAR

RODNEY LAREDO

Those Were The Days ... Series
Alpine Trials & Rallies 1910-1973 (Pfundner)
American 'Independent' Automakers – AMC to Willys 1945 to 1960 (Mort)
American Station Wagons – The Golden Era 1950-1975 (Mort)
American Trucks of the 1950s (Mort)
American Trucks of the 1960s (Mort)
American Woodies 1928-1953 (Mort)
Anglo-American Cars from the 1930s to the 1970s (Mort)
Austerity Motoring (Bobbitt)
Austins, The last real (Peck)
Brighton National Speed Trials (Gardiner)
British and European Trucks of the 1970s (Peck)
British Drag Racing – The early years (Pettitt)
British Lorries of the 1950s (Bobbitt)
British Lorries of the 1960s (Bobbitt)
British Touring Car Racing (Collins)
British Police Cars (Walker)
British Woodies (Peck)
Café Racer Phenomenon, The (Walker)
Don Hayter's MGB Story – The birth of the MGB in MG's Abingdon Design & Development Office (Hayter)
Drag Bike Racing in Britain – From the mid '60s to the mid '80s (Lee)
Dune Buggy Phenomenon, The (Hale)
Dune Buggy Phenomenon Volume 2, The (Hale)
Endurance Racing at Silverstone in the 1970s & 1980s (Parker)
Hot Rod & Stock Car Racing in Britain in the 1980s (Neil)
Last Real Austins 1946-1959, The (Peck)
Mercedes-Benz Trucks (Peck)
MG's Abingdon Factory (Moylan)
Motor Racing at Brands Hatch in the Seventies (Parker)
Motor Racing at Brands Hatch in the Eighties (Parker)
Motor Racing at Crystal Palace (Collins)
Motor Racing at Goodwood in the Sixties (Gardiner)
Motor Racing at Nassau in the 1950s & 1960s (O'Neil)
Motor Racing at Oulton Park in the 1960s (McFadyen)
Motor Racing at Oulton Park in the 1970s (McFadyen)
Motor Racing at Thruxton in the 1970s (Grant-Braham)
Motor Racing at Thruxton in the 1980s (Grant-Braham)
Superprix – The Story of Birmingham Motor Race (Page & Collins)
Three Wheelers (Bobbitt)

General
1½-litre GP Racing 1961-1965 (Whitelock)
AC Two-litre Saloons & Buckland Sportscars (Archibald)
Alfa Romeo 155/156/147 Competition Touring Cars (Collins)
Alfa Romeo Giulia Coupé GT & GTA (Tipler)
Alfa Romeo Montreal – The dream car that came true (Taylor)
Alfa Romeo Montreal – The Essential Companion (Classic Reprint of 500 copies) (Taylor)
Alfa Tipo 33 (McDonough & Collins)
Alpine & Renault – The Development of the Revolutionary Turbo F1 Car 1968 to 1979 (Smith)
Alpine & Renault – The Sports Prototypes 1963 to 1969 (Smith)
Alpine & Renault – The Sports Prototypes 1973 to 1978 (Smith)
Anatomy of the Classic Mini (Huthert & Ely)
Anatomy of the Works Minis (Moylan)
Armstrong-Siddeley (Smith)
Art Deco and British Car Design (Down)
Autodrome (Collins & Ireland)
Autodrome 2 (Collins & Ireland)
Automotive A-Z, Lane's Dictionary of Automotive Terms (Lane)
Automotive Mascots (Kay & Springate)
Bahamas Speed Weeks, The (O'Neil)
Bentley Continental, Corniche and Azure (Bennett)
Bentley MkVI, Rolls-Royce Silver Wraith, Dawn & Cloud/Bentley R & S-Series (Nutland)
Bluebird CN7 (Stevens)
BMC Competitions Department Secrets (Turner, Chambers & Browning)
BMW 5-Series (Cranswick)
BMW Z-Cars (Taylor)
BMW Boxer Twins 1970-1995 Bible, The (Falloon)
BMW Cafe Racers (Cloesen)
BMW Custom Motorcycles – Choppers, Cruisers, Bobbers, Trikes & Quads (Cloesen)
BMW – The Power of M (Vivian)
Bonjour – Is this Italy? (Turner)
British 250cc Racing Motorcycles (Pereira)
British at Indianapolis, The (Wagstaff)
British Café Racers (Cloesen)
British Cars, The Complete Catalogue of, 1895-1975 (Culshaw & Horrobin)
British Custom Motorcycles – The Brit Chop – choppers, cruisers, bobbers & trikes (Cloesen)
BRM – A Mechanic's Tale (Salmon)
BRM V16 (Ludvigsen)
BSA Bantam Bible, The (Henshaw)
BSA Motorcycles – the final evolution (Jones)
Bugatti Type 40 (Price)
Bugatti 46/50 Updated Edition (Price & Arbey)
Bugatti T44 & T49 (Price & Arbey)
Bugatti 57 2nd Edition (Price)
Bugatti Type 57 Grand Prix – A Celebration (Tomlinson)
Caravan, Improve & Modify Your (Porter)
Caravans, The Illustrated History 1919-1959 (Jenkinson)
Caravans, The Illustrated History From 1960 (Jenkinson)
Carrera Panamericana, La (Tipler)
Car-tastrophes – 80 automotive atrocities from the past 20 years (Honest John, Fowler)
Chrysler 300 – America's Most Powerful Car 2nd Edition (Ackerson)
Chrysler PT Cruiser (Ackerson)
Citroën DS (Bobbitt)
Classic British Car Electrical Systems (Astley)
Cobra – The Real Thing! (Legate)
Competition Car Aerodynamics 3rd Edition (McBeath)
Competition Car Composites A Practical Handbook (Revised 2nd Edition) (McBeath)
Concept Cars, How to illustrate and design (Dewey)
Cortina – Ford's Bestseller (Robson)
Cosworth – The Search for Power (6th edition) (Robson)
Coventry Climax Racing Engines (Hammill)
Daily Mirror 1970 World Cup Rally 40, The (Robson)
Daimler SP250 New Edition (Long)
Datsun Fairlady Roadster to 280ZX – The Z-Car Story (Long)
Dino – The V6 Ferrari (Long)
Dodge Challenger & Plymouth Barracuda (Grist)
Dodge Charger – Enduring Thunder (Ackerson)
Dodge Dynamite! (Grist)
Dorset from the Sea – The Jurassic Coast from Lyme Regis to Old Harry Rocks photographed from its best viewpoint (also Souvenir Edition) (Belasco)
Draw & Paint Cars – How to (Gardiner)
Drive on the Wild Side, A – 20 Extreme Driving Adventures From Around the World (Weaver)
Ducati 750 Bible, The (Falloon)
Ducati 750 SS 'round-case' 1974, The Book of the (Falloon)
Ducati 860, 900 and Mille Bible, The (Falloon)
Ducati Monster Bible (New Updated & Revised Edition), The (Falloon)
Ducati 916 (updated edition) (Falloon)
Dune Buggy, Building A – The Essential Manual (Shakespeare)
Dune Buggy Files (Hale)
Dune Buggy Handbook (Hale)
East German Motor Vehicles in Pictures (Suhr/Weinreich)
Fast Ladies – Female Racing Drivers 1888 to 1970 (Bouzanquet)
Fate of the Sleeping Beauties, The (op de Weegh/Hottendorff/op de Weegh)
Ferrari 288 GTO, The Book of the (Sackey)
Ferrari 333 SP (O'Neil)
Fiat & Abarth 124 Spider & Coupé (Tipler)
Fiat & Abarth 500 & 600 – 2nd Edition (Bobbitt)
Fiats, Great Small (Ward)
Fine Art of the Motorcycle Engine, The (Peirce)
Ford Cleveland 335-Series V8 engine 1970 to 1982 – The Essential Source Book (Hammill)
Ford F100/F150 Pick-up 1948-1996 (Ackerson)
Ford F150 Pick-up 1997-2005 (Ackerson)
Ford GT – Then, and Now (Streather)
Ford GT40 (Legate)
Ford Midsize Muscle – Fairlane, Torino & Ranchero (Cranswick)
Ford Model Y (Roberts)
Ford Small Block V8 Racing Engines 1962-1970 – The Essential Source Book (Hammill)
Ford Thunderbird From 1954, The Book of the (Long)
Formula 5000 Motor Racing, Back then ... and back now (Lawson)
Forza Minardi! (Vigar)
France: the essential guide for car enthusiasts – 200 things for the car enthusiast to see and do (Parish)
From Crystal Palace to Red Square – A Hapless Biker's Road to Russia (Turner)
Funky Mopeds (Skelton)
Grand Prix Ferrari – The Years of Enzo Ferrari's Power, 1948-1980 (Pritchard)
Grand Prix Ford – DFV-powered Formula 1 Cars (Robson)
GT – The World's Best GT Cars 1953-73 (Dawson)
Hillclimbing & Sprinting – The Essential Manual (Short & Wilkinson)
Honda NSX (Long)
Inside the Rolls-Royce & Bentley Styling Department – 1971 to 2001 (Hull)
Intermeccanica – The Story of the Prancing Bull (McCredie & Reisner)
Italian Cafe Racers (Cloesen)
Italian Custom Motorcycles (Cloesen)
Jaguar, The Rise of (Price)
Jaguar XJ 220 – The Inside Story (Moreton)
Jaguar XJ-S, The Book of the (Long)
Japanese Custom Motorcycles – The Nippon Chop – Chopper, Cruiser, Bobber, Trikes and Quads (Cloesen)
Jeep CJ (Ackerson)
Jeep Wrangler (Ackerson)
The Jowett Jupiter – The car that leaped to fame (Nankivell)
Karmann-Ghia Coupé & Convertible (Bobbitt)
Kawasaki Triples Bible, The (Walker)
Kawasaki Z1 Story, The (Sheehan)
Kris Meeke – Intercontinental Rally Challenge Champion (McBride)
Lamborghini Miura Bible, The (Sackey)
Lamborghini Urraco, The Book of the (Landsem)
Lambretta Bible, The (Davies)
Lancia 037 (Collins)
Lancia Delta HF Integrale (Blaettel & Wagner)
Land Rover Series III Reborn (Porter)
Land Rover, The Half-ton Military (Cook)
Laverda Twins & Triples Bible 1968-1986 (Falloon)
Lea-Francis Story, The (Price)
Le Mans Panoramic (Ireland)
Lexus Story, The (Long)
Little book of microcars, the (Quellin)
Little book of smart, the – New Edition (Jackson)
Little book of trikes, the (Quellin)
Lola – The Illustrated History (1957-1977) (Starkey)
Lola – All the Sports Racing & Single-seater Racing Cars 1978-1997 (Starkey)
Lola T70 – The Racing History & Individual Chassis Record – 4th Edition (Starkey)
Lotus 18 Colin Chapman's U-turn (Whitelock)
Lotus 49 (Oliver)
Marketingmobiles, The Wonderful Wacky World of (Hale)
Maserati 250F In Focus (Pritchard)
Mazda MX-5/Miata 1.6 Enthusiast's Workshop Manual (Grainger & Shoemark)
Mazda MX-5/Miata 1.8 Enthusiast's Workshop Manual (Grainger & Shoemark)
Mazda MX-5 Miata, The book of the – The 'Mk1' NA-series 1988 to 1997 (Long)
Mazda MX-5 Miata Roadster (Long)
Mazda Rotary-engined Cars (Cranswick)
Maximum Mini (Booij)
Meet the English (Bowie)
Mercedes-Benz SL – R230 series 2001 to 2011 (Long)
Mercedes-Benz SL – W113-series 1963-1971 (Long)
Mercedes-Benz SL & SLC – 107-series 1971-1989 (Long)
Mercedes-Benz SLK – R170 series 1996-2004 (Long)
Mercedes-Benz SLK – R171 series 2004-2011 (Long)
Mercedes-Benz W123-series – All models 1976 to 1986 (Long)
Mercedes G-Wagen (Long)
MGA (Price Williams)
MGB & MGB GT– Expert Guide (Auto-doc Series) (Williams)
MGB Electrical Systems Updated & Revised Edition (Astley)
Micro Caravans (Jenkinson)
Micro Trucks (Mort)
Microcars at Large! (Quellin)
Mini Cooper – The Real Thing! (Tipler)
Mini Minor to Asia Minor (West)
Mitsubishi Lancer Evo, The Road Car & WRC Story (Long)
Montlhéry, The Story of the Paris Autodrome (Boddy)
Morgan Maverick (Lawrence)
Morgan 3 Wheeler – back to the future!, The (Dron)
Morris Minor, 60 Years on the Road (Newell)
Moto Guzzi Sport & Le Mans Bible, The (Falloon)
Motor Movies – The Posters! (Veysey)
Motor Racing – Reflections of a Lost Era (Carter)
Motor Racing – The Pursuit of Victory 1930-1962 (Carter)
Motor Racing – The Pursuit of Victory 1963-1972 (Wyatt/Sears)
Motor Racing Heroes – The Stories of 100 Greats (Newman)
Motorcycle Apprentice (Cakebread)
Motorcycle GP Racing in the 1960s (Pereira)
Motorcycle Road & Racing Chassis Designs (Noakes)
Motorhomes, The Illustrated History (Jenkinson)
Motorsport In colour, 1950s (Wainwright)
MV Agusta Fours, The book of the classic (Falloon)
N.A.R.T. – A concise history of the North American Racing Team 1957 to 1983 (O'Neil)
Nissan 300ZX & 350Z – The Z-Car Story (Long)
Nissan GT-R Supercar: Born to race (Gorodji)
Northeast American Sports Car Races 1950-1959 (O'Neil)
The Norton Commando Bible – All models 1968 to 1978 (Henshaw)
Nothing Runs – Misadventures in the Classic, Collectable & Exotic Car Biz (Slutsky)
Off-Road Giants! (Volume 1) – Heroes of 1960s Motorcycle Sport (Westlake)
Off-Road Giants! (Volume 2) – Heroes of 1960s Motorcycle Sport (Westlake)
Off-Road Giants! (volume 3) – Heroes of 1960s Motorcycle Sport (Westlake)
Pass the Theory and Practical Driving Tests (Gibson & Hoole)
Peking to Paris 2007 (Young)
Pontiac Firebird – New 3rd Edition (Cranswick)
Porsche Boxster (Long)
Porsche 356 (2nd Edition) (Long)
Porsche 908 (Födisch, Neßhöver, Roßbach, Schwarz & Roßbach)
Porsche 911 Carrera – The Last of the Evolution (Corlett)
Porsche 911R, RS & RSR, 4th Edition (Starkey)
Porsche 911, The Book of the (Long)
Porsche 911 – The Definitive History 2004-2012 (Long)
Porsche – The Racing 914s (Smith)
Porsche 911SC 'Super Carrera' – The Essential Companion (Streather)
Porsche 914 & 914-6: The Definitive History of the Road & Competition Cars (Long)
Porsche 924 (Long)
The Porsche 924 Carreras – evolution to excellence (Smith)
Porsche 928 (Long)
Porsche 944 (Long)
Porsche 964, 993 & 996 Data Plate Code Breaker (Streather)
Porsche 993 'King Of Porsche' – The Essential Companion (Streather)
Porsche 996 'Supreme Porsche' – The Essential Companion (Streather)
Porsche 997 2004-2012 – Porsche Excellence (Streather)
Porsche Racing Cars – 1953 to 1975 (Long)
Porsche Racing Cars – 1976 to 2005 (Long)
Porsche – The Rally Story (Meredith)
Porsche: Three Generations of Genius (Meredith)
Preston Tucker & Others (Linde)
RAC Rally Action! (Gardiner)
RACING COLOURS – MOTOR RACING COMPOSITIONS 1908-2009 (Newman)
Racing Line – British motorcycle racing in the golden age of the big single (Guntrip)
Rallye Sport Fords: The Inside Story (Moreton)
Renewable Energy Home Handbook, The (Porter)
Roads with a View – England's greatest views and how to find them by road (Corfield)
Rolls-Royce Silver Shadow/Bentley T Series Corniche & Camargue – Revised & Enlarged Edition (Bobbitt)
Rolls-Royce Silver Spirit, Silver Spur & Bentley Mulsanne 2nd Edition (Bobbitt)
Rootes Cars of the 50s, 60s & 70s – Hillman, Humber, Singer, Sunbeam & Talbot (Rowe)
Rover P4 (Bobbitt)
Runways & Racers (O'Neil)
Russian Motor Vehicles – Soviet Limousines 1930-2003 (Kelly)
Russian Motor Vehicles – The Czarist Period 1784 to 1917 (Kelly)
RX-7 – Mazda's Rotary Engine Sportscar (Updated & Revised New Edition) (Long)
Scooters & Microcars, The A-Z of Popular (Dan)
Scooter Lifestyle (Grainger)
SCOOTER MANIA! – Recollections of the Isle of Man International Scooter Rally (Jackson)
Singer Story: Cars, Commercial Vehicles, Bicycles & Motorcycle (Atkinson)
Sleeping Beauties USA – abandoned classic cars & trucks (Marek)
SM – Citroën's Maserati-engined Supercar (Long & Claverol)
Speedway – Auto racing's ghost tracks (Collins & Ireland)
Sprite Caravans, The Story of (Jenkinson)
Standard Motor Company, The Book of the (Robson)
Steve Hole's Kit Car Cornucopia – Cars, Companies, Stories, Facts & Figures: the UK's kit car scene since 1949 (Hole)
Subaru Impreza: The Road Car And WRC Story (Long)
Supercar, How to Build your own (Thompson)
Tales from the Toolbox (Oliver)
Tatra – The Legacy of Hans Ledwinka, Updated & Enlarged Collector's Edition of 1500 copies (Margolius & Henry)
Taxi! The Story of the 'London' Taxicab (Bobbitt)
To Boldly Go – twenty six vehicle designs that dared to be different (Hull)
Toleman Story, The (Hilton)
Toyota Celica & Supra, The Book of Toyota's Sports Coupés (Long)
Toyota MR2 Coupés & Spyders (Long)
Triumph Bonneville Bible (59-83) (Henshaw)
Triumph Bonneville!, Save the – The inside story of the Meriden Workers' Co-op (Rosamond)
Triumph Motorcycles & the Meriden Factory (Hancox)
Triumph Speed Twin & Thunderbird Bible (Woolridge)
Triumph Tiger Cub Bible (Estall)
Triumph Trophy Bible (Woolridge)
Triumph TR6 (Kimberley)
TT Talking – The TT's most exciting era – As seen by Manx Radio TT's lead commentator 2004-2012 (Lambert)
Two Summers – The Mercedes-Benz W196R Racing Car (Ackerson)
TWR Story, The – Group A (Hughes & Scott)
Unraced (Collins)
Velocette Motorcycles – MSS to Thruxton – New Third Edition (Burris)
Vespa – The Story of a Cult Classic in Pictures (Uhlig)
Vincent Motorcycles: The Untold Story since 1946 (Guyony & Parker)
Volkswagen Bus Book, The (Bobbitt)
Volkswagen Bus or Van to Camper, How to Convert (Porter)
Volkswagens of the World (Glen)
VW Beetle Cabriolet – The full story of the convertible Beetle (Bobbitt)
VW Beetle – The Car of the 20th Century (Copping)
VW Bus – 40 Years of Splitties, Bays & Wedges (Copping)
VW Bus Book, The (Bobbitt)
VW Golf: Five Generations of Fun (Copping & Cservenka)
VW – The Air-cooled Era (Copping)
VW T5 Camper Conversion Manual (Porter)
VW Campers (Copping)
Volkswagen Type 3, The book of the – Concept, Design, International Production Models & Development (Glen)
You & Your Jaguar XK8/XKR – Buying, Enjoying, Maintaining, Modifying – New Edition (Thorley)
Which Oil? – Choosing the right oils & greases for your antique, vintage, veteran, classic or collector car (Michell)
Works Minis, The Last (Purves & Brenchley)
Works Rally Mechanic (Moylan)

www.veloce.co.uk

For post publication news, updates and amendments relating to this book please visit www.veloce.co.uk/books/V5007

First published in October 2016 by Veloce Publishing Limited, Veloce House, Parkway Farm Business Park, Middle Farm Way, Poundbury, Dorchester DT1 3AR, England. Fax 01305 268864 / e-mail info@veloce.co.uk / web www.veloce.co.uk or www.velocebooks.com.

ISBN: 978-1-78711-007-6 UPC: 6-36847-01007-2.

British Library Cataloguing in Publication Data – A catalogue record for this book is available from the British Library. Typesetting, design and page make-up all by Veloce Publishing Ltd on Apple Mac. Printed in India by Replika Press.

A DARRACQ CALLED
GENEVIEVE

THE STORY OF VETERAN MOTORING'S
MOST FAMOUS CAR

RODNEY LAREDO

CONTENTS

AUTHOR'S NOTE. 5

ACKNOWLEDGEMENTS. 7

CHAPTER ONE 9

CHAPTER TWO. 15

CHAPTER THREE. 18

CHAPTER FOUR 22

CHAPTER FIVE 28

CHAPTER SIX 36

CHAPTER SEVEN. 40

CHAPTER EIGHT 44

CHAPTER NINE. 62

CHAPTER TEN. 67

CHAPTER ELEVEN 83

CHAPTER TWELVE. 95

CHAPTER THIRTEEN. 107

CHAPTER FOURTEEN. 119

CHAPTER FIFTEEN 127

CHAPTER SIXTEEN. 133

CHAPTER SEVENTEEN 144

INDEX 159

AUTHOR'S NOTE

I was a very small boy living in Christchurch, New Zealand, when I first watched *Genevieve*. With my mother and two neighbours, I sallied forth to a nearby cinema. The outing was memorable for two reasons; once seated, I was pointedly told *not* to drop the chocolates, as they were handed between the four of us. Unfortunately, I did just that. As the lights dimmed, Roses chocolates could be heard rolling down the sloping wooden floor – carpet was only present in the aisles then – and under the seats in front of us. That was the first reason, and the reprimand that followed, although crushing, was happily short-lived. The second reason was more lasting, and made a huge personal impact on the years that lay ahead, one that I could never have foreseen at the time.

Before me on the screen was a beautiful young woman called Wendy McKim who, with her husband Alan, owned a 1904 French-made Darracq called Genevieve. I was mesmerised by Wendy, her slight aloofness and attractively modulated voice. She became someone I could never forget. Years on, owing to sheer popularity, *Genevieve* would return periodically to many of the new suburban cinemas that were springing up everywhere during the 1960s. I sat and watched the film anywhere it was showing, for I had come to learn that Wendy was played by the actress

Dinah Sheridan, the real object of my interest. My father had a leaning toward old cars, and along the way I picked up his passion; I recall him taking me to *Genevieve* themed gatherings of old 'jalopies,' as he called cars of a certain age.

Later, as an older school boy, I was present at the Addington Showgrounds, in our garden city of Christchurch, to see George and Kathleen Gilltrap check in with Genevieve at the starting point of the 1965 International Rally for Vintage and Veteran Cars. The realisation that I was seeing the famous Darracq in the flesh, so to speak, was awe-inspiring, particularly as my imagination transported me to countless scenes from the movie, with visions of John Gregson and Dinah Sheridan – as Alan and Wendy McKim – sitting up there as driver and passenger in place of the Gilltraps.

Not so many years later, I was given a set of colour transparencies that showed Genevieve against some of the incredible scenery of the South Island, taken during the 1965 International Rally. By then, from whatever sources were available, I had begun to keep a scrapbook of Dinah Sheridan and anything to do with the film that had made her name. What, I wondered, had become of her? Why were there no new films in which she might appear? For all intents and purposes, she had vanished. I wanted to track her down and find out more, but from where, and how?

A weekly English publication at the time offered a service for readers to find out anything about anyone, should they care to write in and ask. Having done so, I received a letter in reply informing me that following *Genevieve*, Dinah Sheridan had put her career on hold for marriage. Undaunted, further research followed and a legitimate plan began to form in my mind. As a secondary school student with a love of comprehension, I hatched the idea of writing a short story on the history of the car that became Genevieve, which the Vintage Car Club of New Zealand had agreed to publish in its magazine *Beaded Wheels*. With this in mind I wrote to Norman Reeves, who owned the Darracq at the time the film was made. He embraced my project, sending a large envelope containing all of the remaining press cuttings and photographs which were still in his keeping, and that didn't need to be returned. The notion that Dinah might be interested in contributing to what I proposed to write spurred me on; this, I convinced myself, was now a 'real' reason to succeed in finding her.

That day finally arrived with a written account from Dinah, detailing some of her memories, which she was only too happy to contribute. As a thank you, I sent in reply some copies of the International Rally transparencies, showing Genevieve being put through her paces. Receiving them coincided with Dinah's own participation in the genuine London to Brighton rally for the first time, and she was able to show her rally companions the images I had sent. Dinah asked me to write again if I wished, and what followed became a unique and special bond spanning several decades, ending only with her eventual departure from this world.

During the intervening years, with her beauty undiminished by age, I was often a welcomed houseguest at her home in London, where in the fullness of time my wife Alethea was also warmly included. The magical day also came when Dinah visited us at our home in New Zealand. We still treasure a photograph of her as she sat in our conservatory, cuddled up to our then two young children, Claire and Andre, to whom she is reading *The Railway Children*. The 1970 film adaptation of the book memorably featured Dinah as the mother, after her career had resumed.

Many years earlier, *Genevieve* had brought us together, and does so again by way of the following pages. Dinah Sheridan outlived those who acted alongside her in this iconic movie. The lives of Kay Kendall and John Gregson ended too early, at just 32 and 55 respectively, prompting Kenneth More to quip, "Well old girl, two down two to go." When his life ended at 68, Dinah, who made it into her 93rd year, spoke for them all when she said:

"Genevieve will be our epitaph."

BY THE SAME AUTHOR

Houses and Gardens of the English Countryside - A Book of Days
The Illustrated International Traveller's Companion
Winter Wellies (a book for children)
To Hell with Poverty

ACKNOWLEDGEMENTS

Most of those who have contributed to this record are no longer with us. Back in late 1993, when Genevieve returned to England after 35 years and went on show at The National Motor Museum in Beaulieu, they were still very much alive. It was because of this that I began to look seriously at putting together an in-depth biography of this celebrated Darracq's life. For several reasons the project didn't move forward, taking until now to see the light of day. My own file of Genevieve history had been continuously added to over the years as information came to hand from a variety of sources. Integral to this was Dinah Sheridan. Not only for playing her role in one of the most memorable of British films, but also for sharing – publicly on numerous occasions, and with me personally over forty years – her memories of doing so.

One of my earliest informants was Norman Reeves, with whom I corresponded some years after Genevieve was no longer his. He sent me what remained of his own memorabilia collection related to the Darracq and said "keep it."

Marjory Cornelius, costume designer for the film *Genevieve*, and whose husband Henry Cornelius produced and directed it, supported the idea of this book, offering her assistance after we first met at The National Motor Museum in November 1993. It was important for her that one day some form of lasting memento to her husband's work should make it into print. At the time of our meeting, she gave me a copy of what cameraman Christopher Challis had recorded and given her, relating to his filming *Genevieve* in Technicolor.

With Marjory Cornelius at Beaulieu was Larry Adler. He gave an entertaining account from his autobiography *It Ain't Necessarily So* (Collins, 1984) on being engaged to play *Genevieve*'s harmonica accompaniment, later talking to me personally about this experience.

Another – welcoming the Darracq's return to the UK – was Tania Rose, whose husband William Rose wrote the film's screenplay. Tania later sent me a copy of the screenplay, along with a background account of how it came to be written in the first place.

I am most grateful to Bill Peacock for sending me, over twenty years ago, an account of being tipped off about the two Darracq chassis in 1945. My appreciation likewise extends to Peter Venning who subsequently took these two wrecks on, and mailed me his version of events. More recently, Bill's daughter Margaret Davies and Peter's son Howard have been supportive with their assistance.

Photographic and written contributions from the distant past provided by Mrs Kathleen Gilltrap have been invaluable. The same can be said of her son George Gilltrap Jnr who I came to know well in Australia. He was generous with his time and in his replies to questions about his family's ownership of Genevieve. Sadly, following his parents, George has now also passed away.

Recognition should be included here for staff members of the Paul Terry Organisation who, back in 1992, were most obliging in supplying copies of promotional material for that years Perth to Albany Genevieve 500.

My thanks are also extended to Cathy Barclay-White, daughter of John Gregson and by coincidence once the nanny to my goddaughter; Elaine Lemon, whose father Frank Reece provided his Spyker as Genevieve's motion picture rival; and Michael Edwards, chairman of the Genevieve 2002 Anniversary Rally. He gave me permission to use material supplied by Marjory Cornelius, covering the production and filming of Genevieve, reproduced in the 2002 anniversary road book, Genevieve – 50 Years On.

My added appreciation goes to The Sydney Morning Herald, The West Australian, TVW7 Perth, Bonhams Auctioneers and Valuers, Benham Coin Covers, Motor Sport magazine, Quirina Louwman, and the Louwman Motor Museum in Holland.

Every reasonable effort has been made to locate likely copyright holders of material reproduced in the pages of this account. Any omissions are unintentional. The author and publishers apologise for that which is not appropriately attributed or remains unattributed.

Lastly, but by no means least, huge thanks go to my wife Alethea, whose hours of background help and advice have been immeasurable.

In Memory of Dinah,
and the friendship of a lifetime

Also as a tribute, to the late
John Gregson, Kay Kendall, and Kenneth More

" *I'm not going with you – this year, next year or any year.*
"*I'll never get into that silly car again.*"

So said an irrate Wendy McKim to her husband Alan the day before Genevieve, their 50 year old Darracq, began her momentous cinematic journey from London to Brighton. The 1953 film of the same name famously takes this annual event, which occurs every November on the first Sunday in the month, as its theme. It is one of the most prestigious events in the British motoring calendar, and draws entrants from all around the world. Its history goes back to 1896, when 'The Emancipation Run' took place to celebrate the abolition of the 2mph speed limit, running from the English capital down to Sussex's south coast. Now, every year, pre-1904 vehicles line up in London's Hyde Park ready to start on their commemorative run to Brighton.

One wonders if Alexandre Darracq ever imagined that an automobile bearing his name would achieve global fame, some half-century after it was introduced to the motoring world.

Born on November 5th 1855 in Bordeaux, France, we know very little of the young Darracq. He began his working life as a draftsman at Tarbes, then moved on to try his hand with Hurtu, a manufacturer of sewing machines. Taking the bull by the horns, in 1891 he teamed up with Jean Aucoc to manufacture bicycles under the name of Gladiator. This proposition became successful to the point where, in 1896, British interests ultimately bought out Darracq and his partner. Two years before, in a factory set up at Suresnes on the outskirts of Paris, the pair had begun experimenting with the newly discovered power of internal combustion, building motor bicycles and quadricycles. They produced the Millet motorcycle, which boasted a 2-litre, 5-cylinder rotary engine built into the back wheel, making it a machine to be reckoned with. What came next, twelve months later, was a light car shown at the Paris Salon. This was then followed up with an experimental electric carriage, which even Darracq had to admit was a washout.

His appetite, however, had not been unduly dampened. Ambitious plans were laid out to venture into car production more seriously, and subsequently hammered home by announcing the production of a varied range of models. For the first few years of the new twentieth century, almost 80 per cent of production line Darracqs were

ADVERTISEMENT SUPPLEMENT TO "THE AUTOCAR," FEBRUARY 18TH, 1904.

DARRACQ CARS

A VISIT TO THE DARRACQ WORKS.

A PEEP INTO THE INNER WORKING OF AN UP-TO-DATE INDUSTRY.

BY A VISITOR.

HAVING arrived in Paris to visit the Automobile Show in December last, I was pleased to find awaiting me a most courteous invitation to visit the works of A. Darracq and Co., Ltd., at Suresnes, which have lately been purchased by the powerful English company at present trading under that name. This invitation I hastened to accept,

being neither noise nor vibration. Passing quickly through the streets, and then through the Bois de Boulogne, we were soon over the river, and, drawing up before the vast Darracq Works on the quay facing the Seine; we were much pleased with the remarkable ease and comfort of our conveyance, the whole distance having been done without any

and accordingly next morning there drew up at my hotel one of the 1904 15 h.p. Darracqs to take myself and party to Suresnes. Having taken our seats, we were surprised to find ourselves immediately in motion, none of us having whilst entering the car realised that the motor was running, there

change of gear, although the speed was varied from upwards of thirty miles an hour in the open down to four or five miles an hour in the traffic.

On entering the works we had the pleasure of a few words with M. Darracq himself, and were afterwards conducted round the works. Passing

[Continued on page 2.]

ILIFFE & SONS LIMITED, LONDON AND COVENTRY.

The Darracq production plant at Suresnes Paris as depicted in The Autocar, Feb 13, 1904.

shipped abroad. A good number of these headed to England, where from 1905 a branch of the company operated as A Darracq 1905 (Ltd) having been set up with a capitalisation of £650,000. By 1912, Englishman Owen Clegg was overseeing design and engineering. His skills had been refined on early Rover cars. By the 1920s the Darracq Company had taken on manufacturing Sunbeam and Talbot vehicles, combining all three to create STD Motors.

Retracing Darracq's infancy allows us to note some interesting milestones. The year 1901 saw Henri Farman win the Pau Auto Race in a modified Voiturette, at the thundering average speed of 39mph. The success of such early races helped Darracq production enormously, and at the end of 1902 the company books showed considerable profit. For the 1903 racing season, Darracq increased its engines to 7.5 litres in order to meet the competition, and from there the pace was set for further success. That same year, he introduced the Arbel chassis which was used on Genevieve. Regarded as a big step forward in metal forming, its creation meant side members and under trays could now be pressed out from one sheet of steel.

In 1905, Victor Hemery drove a 200hp V8 Darracq to a world land speed record of 109.65mph, on the road from Arles to Salon-de-Provence in southern France. Four years later, in 1909, and with the French motor industry at crisis point, Darracq sold its Milan-based Darracq-Italiana works to Anonima Lombarda Fabbrica Automobili (ALFA), which would become Alfa Romeo in 1915.

Malcom Campbell's first Bluebird also had Darracq origins. In 1912, he raced at Brooklands in a 1906 10.5-litre machine bearing the Darracq insignia. Two years earlier, Campbell also tested a Darracq motor known as the 'Flapper.' By the time Genevieve was rolled out in 1904, Darracq's imprint on car manufacturing had become one of the

Continued page 14

1904 12hp 2-cylinder Darracq chassis.

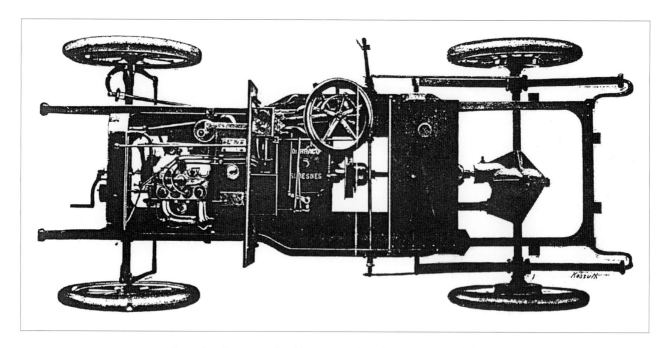

Chassis of 1904 12hp Darracq showing new steel frame.

1904 12hp Darracq engine promoted as having 'many notable improvements which, like women, speak for themselves.'

ADVERTISEMENT SUPPLEMENT TO "THE AUTOCAR," FEBRUARY 13TH, 1904.

Principal Agents in Foreign Countries.

NEW YORK	The American Darracq Automobile Company.
GERMANY	Messrs. Adam, Opel, and Co., Russelsheim.
HOLLAND	Messrs. W. Aertnij & Co., Nimeguen.
ITALY	Messrs. Wehrheim & Co., Torino.
BELGIUM	Messrs. Vandenbroeck & Co., Anvers.
SPAIN	Messrs. Fradera & Co., Barcelona.
PORTUGAL	"Automobilista," Coimbra.
MEXICO	G. O. Braniff & Co., 19, Calle Cadena.
AUSTRALIA	The Knowles Automobile Company, Sydney.
POLAND	Messrs. Lampe & Co., Warsaw.
SOUTH AFRICA	Messrs. J. Garlick & Co., Cape Town.
NEW ZEALAND	The Skeats Company, Auckland.
CHILI	Schloss & Co., Santiago.
CUBA	R. S. Munoz & Co., Havana.
CANADA	R. & W. Kerr, Montreal.

DARRACQ CARS

Can also be obtained from the following Authorised Agents in the

UNITED KINGDOM:

Kent, Surrey, Sussex, and Hants—
H. E. HALL & Co., Tunbridge Wells and Brighton

Nottingham, Leicester, and Lincolnshire—
CHAS. BINKS, LTD., Wollerton St., Nottingham.

Northumberland and Durham—
KIRSOP & Co., Pilgrim Street, Newcastle-on-Tyne.

Liverpool—
WILLIAM LEA, The Motor Car Depot, 16, Berry Street, Liverpool.

Norfolk—
MANN, EGERTON, AND Co., Prince of Wales's Road, Norwich.

Halifax and Huddersfield—
HOYLE BROS., LTD., Brighouse.

Bristol—
BRISTOL WAGON AND CARRIAGE Co., LTD.

Somersetshire—
TAUNTON MOTOR Co., Taunton.

Wilts and Dorset—
J. W. TITT, Warminster.

Suffolk and Colchester—
BOTWOOD & EGERTON, Ipswich.

EastRiding of Yorkshire—
EAST RIDING MOTOR Co., Beverley Road, Hull.

Birmingham—
G. F. HEATH & Co., John Bright Street, Birmingham.

Manchester—
T. GARNER, Peter Street, Manchester.

Devon and Cornwall—
STANDFIELD & WHITE, Exeter.

Swansea—
JOHN S. BROWN, Swansea.

LONDON AGENTS.

London County South of Thames—
G. SKUDDER, Tooley Street, E.C.

Highgate—
THE HIGHGATE MOTOR CAR Co., Grand Parade, Highgate.

Depot for Hire of Darracq Cars—
AUTOMOBILES DE LUXE, 6a, Tudor Street, E.C.

SCOTLAND.

Glasgow, Ayrshire, Renfrewshire, and Dumbartonshire—
KENNEDY MOTOR Co., Cathcart, Glasgow.

IRELAND.

Belfast—
THE NORTHERN MOTOR Co., Montgomery Street, Belfast.

Dublin—
JOHN HUTTON, SONS, AND Co., Summer Hill, Dublin.

WALES.

Montgomery, Radnor, and Brecknock—
MR. TOM NORTON, Llandrindod Wells.

PARIS.   483, OXFORD STREET.   LONDON.

A page from The Autocar, Feb 13, 1904, listing authorised United Kingdom agents for Darracq motorcars.

most significant in the world. Not a driver himself, but forever the entrepreneur, Darracq wasn't slow to recognise that motorsport acted as a catalyst where car sales were concerned, although as a passenger he was ill at ease with speed. In 1904, at Suresnes, the company's Perfecta plant saw the production of some 1600 vehicles. This equated to something approaching 10 per cent of all car production in France at that time. Impressive as that might be, two new models in the range would cause something of a stir for entirely different reasons. Darracq probably had no idea that his fabulous Flying Fifteen – a 3-litre, 4-cylinder, 15hp model – would be an instant success when it was shown to the public for the first time. His other announcement for 1904 was a comparatively insignificant 12hp model. Not even the man himself would have entertained the idea that such a model would bring fame and fortune to the Darracq

name, many years after both he and his motoring empire were long gone. Nevertheless such was the fate of this car, which measured at just 9ft 6in long by 4ft 8in wide, with its twin vertical cylinders, 120mm bore and 110mm stroke. Unique for the period, because it was attached to the steering column, was the gearlever, which offered three forward and one reverse gear. The model came with battery and trembler coil ignition, cone clutch transmission, live axle with cut bevel for final drive, internal expanding brakes on the rear with a foot brake on the front, and – in favourable conditions – a capability of 40mph. Darracq believed that here, at last, was his own attempt to provide motoring pleasure to 'Mr Average.'

Genevieve was shipped to Darracq Motors in Oxford Street, London, five years into the 20th century. It was from here that her wheels began to roll toward immortality.

CHAPTER TWO

Just over 40 years later, in 1945, a court bailiff called Bill Bailey was in the process of serving a court order along the Lea Bridge Road in Leyton, East London. Bailey, who was also a renowned enthusiast and collector of old motorcycles, accidentally struck his shin on a piece of iron protruding from a hedge; looking behind the foliage, he found a derelict builder's yard lying slightly below street level. Investigating, he discovered, to his utter amazement, roughly fifteen very old cars partially covered beneath the debris of bricks, chimney pots, and similar items. Bailey passed the news of his discovery on to his friends Bill Peacock and Jack Wadsworth, both veteran car collectors.

In October 1993, an article appeared in *The Daily Telegraph* stating that Genevieve was being returned to England after more than three decades, to be sold to the highest bidder. In response, Bill Peacock wrote to the *Telegraph*'s motoring editor, and also to Brookes the auctioneer, suggesting it was high time that the Darracq's early history – where known – should be put on record for the benefit of the new owner.

The portion of Darracq chassis protruding from the Leyton hedge led to an astonishing hoard that, in present day terms, would have fetched astronomical sums of money for those lucky enough to be in on the find. Upon further investigation of a pile of rubble closest to the footpath, Bill discovered the remains of a 1903/04 French-built Darracq complete with all major components, albeit with anything removable long gone. Probing more deeply into the yard revealed another, almost completely buried, Darracq of the same vintage. Sleeping peacefully alongside were found two chassis belonging to a couple of Renault 8/10 taxis dating to 1909/10. One had the vestige of a body still intact, while the other had been completely stripped. Both were apparently the same type of vehicles as those used to cart French reinforcements during World War One's Battle of the Marne. The better of the two cars wasn't in such poor condition, apart from some grime and flat tyres, and – amazingly – could eventually be started. Close by, almost obscured by rubbish, was a 10/12hp Argyll with a four-seater rear-entry tonneau body. This car was complete and in good order, except for some offside rot. Bill Peacock put his name on it and ultimately, following a two year restoration, this find became a frequent entry in the annual London to Brighton run, following acceptance by the Veteran Car Club as a fully recognised 1903 model.

Another discovered prize of the same year proved to be a 12hp Sunbeam. Jack Wadsworth,

1947, showing left-to-right: the 1903 Argyll found in the builders yard with the two Darracqs, Frank Reece's restored 1904 Dutch Spyker, and an 1898 Daimler en route to London's Regent Park.

already a Sunbeam fan, nabbed this rarity to pair up with a 16hp 1931 Sunbeam saloon he had purchased sometime before. This car was subsequently put into service as a towing vehicle, used to transport all the movable finds in the yard across London. One of these happened to be a large tourer, its front end totally obscured by rubbish when first found. Once cleared, it was exposed as a 18hp Thornycroft from 1910/11. Like the other cars around it, the Thorny had been idle for an unknown number of years, but with air in the tyres and fresh petrol she started on the first try. Later, this car was run as found in a Veteran Car Club rally. The organisers and other participants, however, didn't see the funny side; for those who felt it should have been restored, it was a painful sight.

A further interesting discovery proved to be something of a headache. From its appearance, it was quite clear that this find dated back to very early models; it had solid-tyred rear wheels which were larger than the front, a chain-driven 4-cylinder Aster engine, and exposed timing wheels. The cylinders were T-headed castings, with valves and camshafts at each side of the engine. The body was a wagonette with a bench front seat separated from the rear, which had seats running fore and aft. The sides of the rear part of the body were carried on turned wooden spindles, also used on early governess pony traps.

There was no name on the radiator, but the rear hubcaps were marked with the name Whitlock Aster, whilst the front caps were engraved with Withers. Whitlock Aster had its beginnings in the dim and distant past, and by the mid-1940s no trace could be found. Withers, on the other hand, were still operating from premises on Edgware Road. What happened to this vehicle is not known. The same can be said about some of the other discoveries, although the uniqueness of the Whitlock Aster means that it was likely the last of its kind, and really should have been preserved.

A very early Morris, from about 1913, was likewise found amongst the debris. This was fitted with what was truly a Hotchkiss engine, as opposed to the type later used for 'bull nose' models and wrongly attributed to Hotchkiss. It didn't have a dyno starter (as was fitted to later models), instead only offering a handle to get it going, and had rather small-section beaded-edge wheels. There were also three cars on their own, set somewhat away from all the others, and clear of the accumulated jumble of tiles and chimney pots that had been their sleeping companions for so long. One was a Daimler Landaulet, from perhaps 1912 or thereabouts. There was a two-seater 10hp Singer of similar vintage, familiar as a World War One officers' transport. Finally, there was a Ford Model T tourer with wire wheels. Messrs Peacock and Wadsworth lived to regret vandalising the Daimler by removing the cylinder blocks from the sleeve-valve engine; a friend had put out a plea for spare blocks of a similar type, the better to complete an engine restoration on his own Daimler.

Another threesome worthy of mention comprised a complete 1910/11 Humber taxi, a Mercedes saloon of 1921 vintage – complete with a curvaceous body typical of the period, and a full compliment of bevelled glass to go with it – and a mid-1920s square-backed Essex Super Six. The Humber proved a handful in more ways than one; having managed to roll it onto the road and across the pavement, ready to manhandle it onto the carrier, a cracking sound was heard, preceding the total disintegration of all four wheels as the spokes simply fell apart.

CHAPTER
THREE

The owner of the derelict builders yard, and by extension the amazing collection of elderly motors, turned out to be something of a recluse. However, over a period of time he began to thaw. When he did open up, it transpired that he had – at some point – been an engineer on the Argentinian railways, but by 1945 was residing in the scullery of his junk-filled house attached to the Lea Bridge Road property. While negotiations were under way to purchase this rare collection of cars, Bill Peacock sought out the owner – whose name seemed to be Rouse or Rowse – by following a rubbish-lined pathway to his kitchen door. Looking inside, he could see it was full of debris reaching up to the ceiling, and once entry had been gained the rest of the house was found to be no better. Finally, Peacock and Wadsworth made a deal with the owner, totalling the princely sum of £45 for the purchase of the entire stash of vehicles. Those that weren't sold on as found, or where they stood, were hauled onto trailers over several weekends – with the help of an army of naive friends – and carted off to be split between Bill Peacock's Chiswick garden and Jack Wadsworth's property in Isleworth.

The towing procedure to get these ancient cars across London, from Leyton to Isleworth, became something of a herculean exercise. Even though the war in Europe was over, fuel rationing most certainly wasn't; as a result, a great deal of fiddling and diddling had to take place to secure the petrol coupons needed. A certain policeman was always stationed on point duty outside the Bank of England, and watched with a wry look on his face as one decrepit wreck after another was paraded before him – week after week – on their journey across the capital. Apparently, his loudly expressed comments over the successive weeks were as priceless as that which trundled past.

The two Darracqs with hardly a body between them ended up in Isleworth as well. The one found lying closest to the Lea Bridge Road footpath showed greater promise than the other, which was certainly more complete but severely rusted. Front wheels on each had rotted away, as had the front dumb irons on the more recognisable of the cars. Reputedly, both Darracqs were subsequently hocked off for £25 to a collector by the name of Peter Venning, newly married and living in the Hertfordshire village of Takeley. By his own account it was he, Peter, who embarked on the initial task of creating one vehicle from two, and getting it into roadworthy condition. To do so required dismantling both wrecks, then reassembling a – more or less – rolling chassis on the one sound frame. Once mobile it was towed to a nice dry shed at Cannons Farm, near Start Hill and not far from Venning's home.

Before this stage had been reached, something unusual occurred; the future casting its own shadow, as it were. One Sunday morning, while Peter Venning was stripping down the two Darracqs in the Isleworth yard, Jack Wadsworth drove in with another veteran on a trailer. Offloading it, he announced "Got a rare one here, found it behind Swann's Motors in Brentford."

Despite being in an advanced state of decay, this particular find was virtually complete. The Reece brothers of Shepherd's Bush, who ran a taxi fleet, later took ownership of it and went on to restore their purchase magnificently.

A few short years later, two immaculately restored vehicles would meet up side-by-side on a film set. The dilapidated car brought into the Isleworth yard on a trailer that Sunday morning was destined to become Genevieve's on screen sparring partner, the bright daffodil yellow Dutch Spyker!

While dismantling the Darracqs appears to have begun in Isleworth, assembling what parts there were took place in a borrowed workshop near Kew Bridge, which Venning had been offered the use of. Within the space of twelve months the engine was stripped, cleaned, and reassembled; this included the gearbox and back axle, which collectively made up the most serviceable components. The engine at this point was created from what came off the rusted chassis, and not from the more complete car which (according to Peter Venning) had nothing that could be called an engine at all. There is, though, a variance of opinion here. Further down the track, when Bill Peacock heard the Darracq had been sold to Norman Reeves, he contacted the new owner offering him an engine, gearbox and axles, et cetera, from what he believed was the rusted chassis. Along with this

offer, however, went a radiator. This is curious to a degree, as there's no record of what this radiator was like, or where it came from. Could it have been any different – better even – than the stack-tube (indicating a car of an earlier period) which was already on the vehicle when Peter hauled it out to Hertfordshire? If Bill Peacock's recollections are correct, these mechanical parts would be the same that first propelled the Darracq along during its initial restoration period. So, where did they come from?

Back near Kew Bridge, everything necessary had been fitted to the sound chassis frame, and temporary rigs were in place for the ignition and carburettor. Finally, the engine was set running. The back axle turned, and even the clutch and gear change could be activated. One might have assumed that this all took place in the Kew workshop but, in a letter to the author some years later, Bill Peacock (writing from his home in Spain) described what became of the collection of cars, as originally found. He wrote, "the Sunbeam was taken over by friend J Wadsworth for his use, and we set about building one sound chassis out of the two Darracqs. The newly assembled car first ran in the garden of the house in Chiswick where I was then living."

Bill's wording would seem to give rise to a question over the order of events at that time. Interestingly enough, a few months after Bill Peacock wrote to *The Daily Telegraph*, Peter Venning also put pen to paper, detailing his view on the origins of the car which became Genevieve. This account was later published in *Motor Sport*, but Peter also wrote to me directly spelling out his recollections. As if to hammer home his point, he quoted Socrates, saying "truth is absolute, it requires not the qualification of belief."

Peter believed he was a stickler for the truth, making no bones about the Darracq propelled

to movie stardom as being something of a composite, made up of bits from here and there, foreign wheels, and a body from an unknown make. His memories run along similar lines to Peacock's recollections, albeit with a significant difference; the implication is given by Peter that the car couldn't have travelled anywhere – even the short distance within a Chiswick garden – because it didn't have a set of wheels. It had back wheels, yes, and with perfectly fitting tyres. However, the front set weren't acquired until a later date. According to Peter, he was passing a chicken farm beneath Dunstable Downs, in Bedfordshire, when he spotted an old Ford Model T This car had wooden wheels of the correct size, and was in sound condition, so Peter bought the wheels for just a few shillings. When matched with the Darracq's hubs, however, it was discovered that while the hubs fitted over the centre boss, the holes didn't coincide with those on the wheels. As a result, Peter proceeded to drill another set which did. What is not 100 per cent certain is whether these wheels were found before the car left Kew, or after it was towed to the Vennings' home in Hertfordshire.

Bill Peacock drives a four-seater 1904 Darracq (believed to be a Flying Fifteen) in 1949, with Peter Venning as passenger.

CHAPTER
FOUR

Next was the body restoration, and the question became whether to find a suitable body or to build one. For Peter Venning, providence yet again came to his aid. His landlord, old farmer Cannon, passed by one day and enquired as to what kind of body he intended to attach, presuming something suitable could be found. "That's the problem," came the reply. "I've got to find something that will fit, and is restorable." The farmer then embarked on a long-winded explanation about how, years ago in the early days of motoring, he had owned a car. When it ceased to run, he had removed the body and mounted it on wheels so it could be turned into a gig and pulled along by his favourite mare, Flower. Eventually the gig was retired, moving to a barn which happened to be close to the Vennings' Takeley residence, near Start Hill. After a long search in the gloom of said barn, the gig was found lying on its side and partially covered in debris; filthy, but quite sound.

Having cut the body bolts from the frame, this newly found treasure was ceremoniously carried across to the shed where the Darracq was being restored, and carefully placed on the chassis. Remarkably, the width of the chassis, body bearers, and dashboard were all the same.

By 1947 the car was sufficiently advanced in its restoration to warrant being registered with the authorities. It was at this point that the registration number HXR 322 was issued, later appearing on the registration papers handed to the next owner, and attached to the car in the film. Over the years there has been much consternation regarding this registration, but Peter always maintained – quite adamantly – that verification of HXR 322 could be obtained for anyone curious enough to request it.

It was at this point that Peter Venning, as a young married man, reluctantly faced up to the fact that he possessed neither the facilities nor the money necessary to complete the Darracq's rebuilding programme as he would have wished. Towards the end of 1949, he placed an advertisement in the 'For Sale' column of *Motor Sport* magazine. The ad offered the Darracq as partly-restored, complete with new tyres, tubes, spare engine, gearbox, and back axle – but requiring a new 'stack tube' radiator – all for £35!

Norman Reeves, a Ford dealer from Uxbridge in Middlesex, responded to the advert and became

Opposite: The page from late 1949 in Motor Sport, carrying the advert Peter Venning placed to sell his 1904 Darracq. Left hand column, eighth item down.

the Darracq's new owner. In his own words, he recalled that they "brought the thing back in bits and pieces, having shovelled up a good deal of it, putting what was shovelled into boxes." Reeves had taken over his business from his father Albert Reeves, whose Ford dealership had at one point been the second largest in the country. The joint Managing Director at the business, a Major Henry Fairhurst, also enjoyed a passion for old cars and was the proud owner of an 1898 Decauville. Norman was keen to expand his own collection, which at that point consisted of two early Benz models, a rare Durkopp, and a green 1903 6hp two-seater De Dion Bouton, known as the 'Iver Flyer,' or more frequently as the 'Menace.' Interestingly enough, and indeed some time before the Reeves Darracq had been earmarked for stardom, Albert Reeves' daughter Margaret Alberta Johnston (a half-sister of Norman's) recalled her father offering the De Dion for use in a film. The film was to be made featuring a collection of veteran cars, and to be called *Genevieve* after the patron saint of Paris. It is worth noting that in the original draft of William Rose's movie screenplay, the starring car is referred to as being a De Dion.

Charlie Cadby, who worked for Reeves, was given the task of completing the Darracq's restoration. Between them, Cadby and Norman Reeves cobbled together parts from another 1904 12hp model, which more than likely came from the remains of the second rusted Darracq, rescued from Leyton and handed over by Bill Peacock. Further help was enlisted from Bob Gregory, the owner of a well-known 1904 Darracq Flying Fifteen. This was the car that, in 1949, had been driven 760 miles from Brighton, on England's

Bob Gregory's 1904 Darracq, from which Norman Reeves' restorer Charlie Cadby copied the radiator style for the Motor Sport purchase.

From 1950/51, showing Reeves' newly restored Darracq, known then as 'Annie,' complete with gig seat originally found by Peter Venning.

southern coast, to John O'Groats at the northern extremity of Scotland. Gregory agreed to loan his car to Reeves, from which a radiator pattern could be taken to replace the tubular version then in place. Duplicating this for the Reeves restoration was not technically correct – when speaking about authenticity – but distinctive nonetheless. Luckily, most of the basic mechanical specs of Charlie Cadby's inherited project were in accordance with those used in 1904. These included a tubular front axle, an aluminium crankcase, and bronze rear brake shoes. This helped move the car closer to approval from the Veteran Car Club's dating authority, and ultimate acceptance as a legitimate participant in the annual London to Brighton

Veteran Car Run. Hesitation still existed, however; the radiator design in particular was a sticking point, and the club pointed out that the push-forward pedals were certainly from 1905, and piano-style replacements from 1904 would have to be found. These were acquired, along with a few other genuine extras, resulting in an eventual thumbs up from the club.

By 1950, the car – now given the name 'Annie' – was ready for its first continental excursion, to Le Touquet in France. With Norman Reeves at the wheel, the 40-mile run from Calais was completed in just over two hours. Twelve months later, both car and owner visited Paris, and were featured on the front page of *Le Matin*. A 500-mile

This photo also comes from the 1950/51 period, but interestingly 'Annie' has a seating arrangement with a lower back, which differs from the gig look.

run to Liège was also successfully undertaken. Despite all of this, Reeves was not a happy man. Back in England, and wrestling with his Darracq's appearance, Norman placed himself once more in the hands of Charlie Cadby. Cadby reasoned that the car's character could be enhanced by replacing the buggy-style seating. Achieving this meant installing a decorative twin-bench 'tulip' design, covered in red leather, which would provide a more authentically high back, while also allowing for space behind to accommodate a slightly sloping boot box with a lifting lid. The steering wasn't all that attractive either; Cadby altered the camber, hoping Annie would drive as well in a straight line as she did when turning corners.

CHAPTER
FIVE

Releases of the film *Genevieve* over the past few decades have helped to keep it in the minds of cinema and television audiences around the globe. The story is as topical now as it was in the early 1950s; perhaps there are some present day London to Brighton participants for whom the reality of the screen adaptation can run a bit too close for comfort!

In 1950, as that year's 54-mile annual London to Brighton Veteran Car Run got under way, the Veteran Car Club of Great Britain's membership was sparse, its coffers equally so. At the same time, American screenwriter William Rose (*It's a Mad, Mad, Mad, Mad World*; *Guess Who's Coming to Dinner*; et cetera) was living with his English wife and infant daughter in a Sussex cottage close to the A23, the main route for the run.

Rose, who happened to be out walking his dog, conceived the outline of a story as he watched the cars pass close to his cottage. That story would become *Genevieve*, one of the most famous motion pictures in the history of the British film industry, and one of the most commercially successful comedies ever to emerge from the studios of the mammoth Rank Organisation. The film also turned out to be a much-needed stimulus for not only the Veteran Car Club of Great Britain, but for veteran motoring clubs worldwide.

William Rose's whimsical storyline concerned, at the basic level, a rollicking romp between two young couples who, having successfully – albeit hilariously, by way of numerous hiccups – made it to Brighton in their ancient cars, hatch a plan to race them back to London the next day. Much bickering surrounds this and a wager of £100 is made, to be given to the owner of the first car over Westminster Bridge. For those not conversant with the screenplay, the following synopsis from J Arthur Rank's promotional material, dated May 1953, will explain further:

Alan McKim (John Gregson) a young barrister, is the proud possessor of a veteran car. Genevieve, a 1904 Darracq, is the apple of his eye. But Alan's rosy view of Genevieve is not shared by his pretty wife, Wendy (Dinah Sheridan), who is unable to appreciate the finer feelings of the motor enthusiast. The day before the annual London to Brighton commemoration rally, Alan is tuning up Genevieve, when Ambrose Claverhouse (Kenneth More), an old friend of Wendy's, arrives in a Dutch Spyker, also 1904 vintage.

Claverhouse, a wealthy advertising agent and confirmed bachelor, passes rude remarks about Alan's car and precipitates a row between Alan and his wife. The next day, Genevieve and dozens

An original Genevieve cinema poster.

of other veterans set off for Brighton. Claverhouse is accompanied by his latest girlfriend, Rosalind Peters (Kay Kendall), a dazzling beauty.

For the McKims the journey to the coast is one of progressive disaster. After five previous rallies, Wendy is a resigned and none too willing passenger. She considers the whole affair childish. When the McKims arrive in Brighton, it is already dark. They failed to complete the journey in the appointed time, owing to a stupid mistake, and have no accommodation. As a consequence they have to stay at an uncomfortable and ancient hotel. But Ambrose and Rosalind have made the journey in fine style and are eventually joined by Wendy and Alan at a Brighton nightclub. While dancing with Wendy, Ambrose confides that although he has taken a different girl on the rally each year, he never succeeded in having any subsequent 'romance.' With Rosalind, however, his hopes were high. But Rosalind announces brusquely that she will play the trumpet. She borrows one from the band, plays with great virtuosity, and passes out to the intense mortification of Ambrose.

Back at the hotel, Alan is morose. He has become unreasonably jealous of Ambrose's easy familiarity with his wife; and Wendy, smiling enigmatically, does little to allay his suspicions. Later, the two men, both disappointed in love, meet in the garage where their cars are parked. Unwisely, Claverhouse makes one of his characteristic digs at Genevieve. Alan is furious. Although he owns the slower car, he challenges Ambrose to a race back to London. Their vanity touched, the price rises steadily until they finally agree to wager one hundred pounds on which car will be first to reach Westminster Bridge, a bet Alan can ill afford to lose.

Continued page 32

Alan McKim trying to convince his reluctant wife, Wendy, that she should join him again for their annual jaunt from London to Brighton.

The Genevieve stars and their cars. (Photo by ITV/REX/Shutterstock)

Next morning the two cars head for London, both Wendy and Rosalind convinced that their menfolk have gone crazy. The journey is packed with surprises, and develops with alarming pace into a motorist's free-for-all, in which the rival drivers do everything to win the race short of draining the petrol from each other's tanks. In a thrilling finish *Genevieve* proves herself the winner. Alan realises that his fears about Wendy have been groundless, and the two couples are reunited.

At the time, William Rose was broke. There had been no work for two years, and he and his wife Tania had decided to part until things improved. Accepting a barman's job in a Devonshire village pub, Rose meant to write by day and work in the evening.

Whilst these arrangements were being made, Rose's screenplay for *Genevieve* had been doing the rounds of the production companies. Eight producers turned it down before South African-born Henry Cornelius picked it up to become both producer and director.

Cornelius had previously been an established director based at Ealing Studios, famous for films showcasing its own brand of cinematic humour known as the Ealing Comedies. He had already scored considerable success with films such as *It Always Rains on Sundays*, *Passport to Pimlico* and *The Galloping Major*, but had since resigned from Ealing to go independent.

Michael Balcon, head of production at Ealing, was aware that *Genevieve* could be a success, but unfortunately found that an overbooked filming schedule meant he could not offer Cornelius floor space in the Ealing Studios for production. Reluctantly, he suggested trying Earl St John at the Rank Organisation's Pinewood Studios, Ealing's direct opposition.

St John was less than enthusiastic, going so far as to tell Cornelius that if he sanctioned the production of 'that sort of film' he would be sacked on the spot and, frankly, he couldn't afford to lose his job.

Cornelius' late wife Marjory recalled:

"*Genevieve* was nearly not made by my husband, Henry Cornelius. He had been working on a comedy to be called *The Little Four*, at the offices of Alexander Korda, who had promised to help finance the film. On this particular morning there was a meeting, and it was decided not to proceed with the film, because the story was based on the world political situation; the Big Four, England, France, Russia and the USA at that time were unable to come to any agreement on how to maintain peace in the world, and four totally unimportant little people from these countries got together to see whether they couldn't work things out and put matters into perspective. The reason for deciding to drop the film was that the

world situation had so further deteriorated that it was felt it was inappropriate to make a comedy of this serious matter.

"My husband returned to his office feeling very depressed, and started to clear his desk, his work being over at Alexander Korda's. On the desk were some scripts that had been sent to him, all neatly bound. In his depressed state, he told his secretary to return them all to their writers. As he passed the thick scripts over, a small sheaf of typewritten papers dropped out, about ten pages of double-spaced quarto-sized. He glanced at the first page.

"The next thing was that I received a telephone call from my husband at our home in Ealing. 'Come up to town right away,' he said. As we were preparing to move house in the next few days, I told him that this just wasn't on. 'Get into a taxi and come.' When I arrived at his office, he pushed the little bundle over to me and said, 'Read.' When I had finished, I said, 'That is your next film, isn't it?' 'You really think so?' ... 'Absolutely.' He said, 'Shall we put all our money into it?' 'Absolutely.'"

Cornelius returned on three occasions to persuade Earl St John, who finally agreed to provide 70 per cent of the small £115,000 budget if Henry Cornelius could source the remaining 30 per cent. This he did with the help of the government-sponsored merchant bank, the National Film Finance Corporation.

Back in Sussex, William and Tania Rose had sold everything they owned, except their bed and refrigerator. Then, the evening before he was due to leave for Devon, Rose's agent telephoned to say that Henry Cornelius wanted to see him.

Rose had, in fact, never written a film before. Previously, he had only rewritten parts of – and made adjustments to – other people's work, in order to suit directors, producers, and

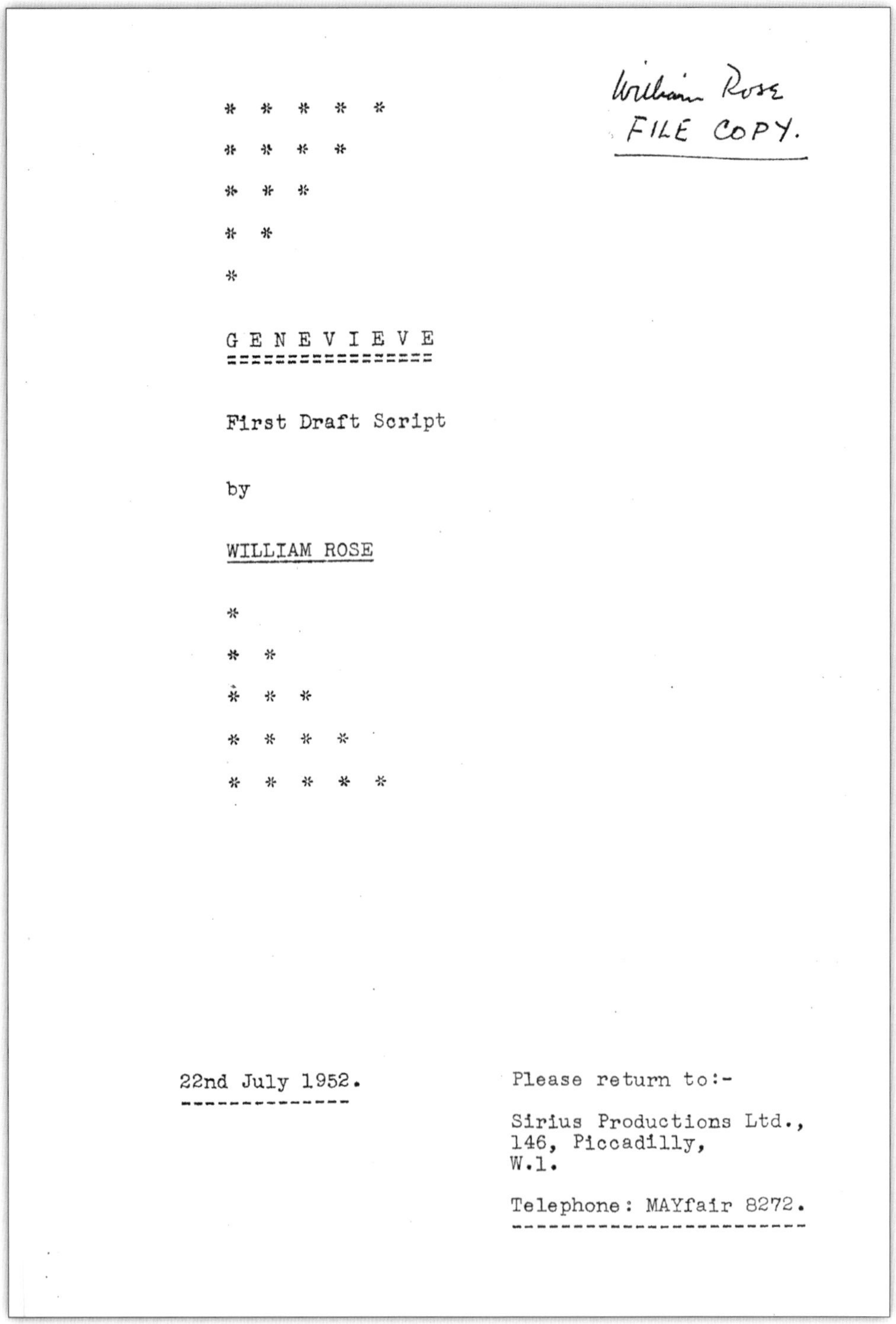

William Rose
FILE COPY.

```
*   *   *   *   *

*   *   *   *

*   *   *

*   *

*
```

G E N E V I E V E
==================

First Draft Script

by

WILLIAM ROSE

```
*

*   *

*   *   *

*   *   *   *

*   *   *   *   *
```

22nd July 1952.

Please return to:-

Sirius Productions Ltd.,
146, Piccadilly,
W.1.

Telephone: MAYfair 8272.

William Rose's first draft of his Genevieve screenplay, dated July 22nd 1952.
Filming began in September of the same year.

uncooperative stars. Greeting Henry Cornelius, he quipped, "I suppose you want to alter the story beyond all recognition." "Not at all," replied Corny (as he was known in the industry), "we will work together so that both of us are in total agreement with the result," which they did.

Marjory Cornelius gives a further insight:

"Bill and my husband worked splendidly together, and their script meetings were comedies in themselves. We had a flat near Marble Arch, where they met. One day my husband, in response to some remark Bill made, said that the British were so well-mannered that no matter how strange a person walked down a street, people would never stop and stare or make loud remarks ... they would only just glance. 'I don't believe it,' said Bill. 'Absolutely,' said my husband. 'Prove it,' said Bill. After a little thought, my husband, with my help, burned a cork, and he made himself huge eyebrows and moustache. I curled his hair into a bush, and with a cigar, pronounced himself Groucho Marx and ready to go. I drove them down to Oxford Street and, near Selfridges, they got out of the car, and my husband started loping along in an imitation of Groucho Marx, but more exaggerated. I drove slowly behind. Not a soul did more than glance quietly in surprise. When eventually I stopped the car for them to get in, a man did come up very politely and said, 'Could I have your autograph, Mr Marx?' We laughed all the way home."

Corny explained to Rose that the budget would be tight, and that all he could offer for the screenplay would be £750. Desperate for money, Rose agreed to this, waiving the other option of a 25 per cent share in any profits the film might make.

CHAPTER
SIX

William Rose was a fast worker. Following each discussion with Cornelius, he would go home and write the part of the script which had been picked over and have it ready by the next day.

That the film was to be made in colour added further considerations, and costly ones at that. Christopher Challis, responsible for the Technicolor photography, has recorded the following:

"One day, while having an overdue holiday with my family in Cornwall, I was contacted by George Gunn of Technicolor, who told me that he had a very interesting project to put before me and asked if I would care to come up for a meeting on the following Monday. Reluctantly abandoning one of the rare chances of a normal break together, I decided to find out what it was all about.

"Henry Cornelius had been, for a long time, trying to raise financing for a picture called *Genevieve*, written around the veteran car race from London to Brighton. He had approached in turn all the major distributors, who had turned it down, expressing the general feeling that it was a subject with little appeal to the average cinemagoer. Finally, the Rank Organisation had agreed to back it, but with the minimum investment, and on condition that Henry Cornelius put up the completion money himself. In order to do this, he had mortgaged his house and sold every tangible asset and here he was, with the absolute minimum of finance, on the verge of turning his dream into a reality.

"George Gunn had persuaded him that, in spite of the money problem, the extra cost of filming in colour was more than worthwhile as, at that time, it was a great attraction at the box office. Planned to be filmed almost entirely outdoors, with a starting date in mid-October, weather was obviously a big hazard, and Henry explained that he could not afford to wait for ideal conditions. 'If there is enough light to get a bare exposure, I just have to shoot. I know it's asking a lot, but there is no other way I can make the picture. Go away and read the script and if you feel you want to take it under these conditions, I will promise that if any money is left at the end, I will try and retake anything that is a particular disaster.' He had written the script himself, in collaboration with Bill Rose, and of course it was marvellous. I knew immediately that I had to do it, no matter the problems, and to this day I do not understand why the backers could not see its potential.

September 17th, 1952. Joined by co-stars on location, Dinah Sheridan cuts her 32nd birthday cake while seated in the Spyker. (Photo by ITV/REX/Shutterstock)

"Photographically it presented a complete break with tradition. Convention dictates that, just as actors should look flawless, so should the world in which they lived be bathed in eternal sunshine. I had felt for a long time that colour photography looked very much better than black and white in flat light conditions, and that the high contrast between highlight and shadow in sunlight was often a disadvantage. There was no time or money available for extensive tests. It was a straight 'yes' or 'no' to the offer, and with the challenge and the opportunity, it had to be 'yes.'

"This period coincided with the ascendancy of the accountants, and the management had become deeply involved with a process known as 'independent frame.' Briefly, the idea was to replace conventional sets with a projected background, both still and moving. A small piece of set was then constructed, where the actors performed, which interlocked exactly with the projected background. In theory, the need for large sets was over. You just went along and photographed the drawing room of a stately home or the interior of a church and all that was needed was a pulpit or a foreground settee to complete the illusion. In practice, it meant tying down the camera height, movement, and choice of lens months before filming commenced, which was obviously impractical and totally unacceptable to any creative director. Several million pounds were spent on rear projection equipment, hydraulic towers and lighting rails, yet only a few significant films were ever made using the process and a great deal of the equipment was finally scrapped.

"The spin-off was the rear projection system, which was by far the best in Europe. In *Genevieve*, nearly half the script consisted of scenes between two people driving along in the old cars: the perfect situation for back-projection. We were unable, for reasons of internal accountancy, to use the facilities which were standing idle in the studio financing the film. The same situation existed with regard to the sound stages and our interiors had to be cut to a bare minimum on the basis of cost.

"As an example, the garage scene in Brighton was shot in two adjoining lock-up garages belonging to the studio transport department, a communicating hole being knocked in the wall and a large tarpaulin extension erected to keep out the light and extend the area. The travelling scenes in the cars were resolved by loading the whole unit into a large flat, open trailer, known as the Queen Mary. It was a relic of the war, and had been used to transport military aircraft. We all piled in – camera, lights, crew, and a small generator – and on the back was perched a mock-up of

A great marketing shot of Genevieve with John Gregson and Dinah Sheridan.
(Photo by ITV/REX/Shutterstock)

the car in which our actors 'drove.' The whole circus was at the mercy of the driver in the cab of the Queen Mary, who often proved difficult to communicate with. Another truck followed with mock-ups of the other cars, ready to be switched at a moment's notice. For forward-looking shots, another flat truck was used. The driving cab was removed, further mock-ups made to disguise what little we saw of the bonnet, and a period steering wheel and windscreen fitted, all of which had to be changed each time we switched cars. For the forward-looking shot, the unit perched on the back and the actor in question had to drive. A slight drawback occurred on the first day, when it was discovered that John Gregson could not drive and, anyway, needed a goods vehicle licence. He was rushed off on an intensive driving course while we occupied ourselves for a couple of days, and the question of the goods licence was met by ignoring it.

"Everything was shot within a few miles of the studio, because of the short days and the expense. We would set off each morning, regardless of the weather, and take advantage of whatever turned up, often asking an astonished local if he or she knew of a water-splash, a sharp left hand bend or a small pub with a courtyard, depending on what requirements had been forced on us by the weather and ever-changing schedule. Henry asked me every few minutes if there was still enough light to shoot, a situation I resolved by giving him an exposure meter on which I drew a red line indicating the point of no return. More than half the scenes were shot with the needle hovering over the line, or even a bit under it, for we all shared the will to make it work. The artists, Kenneth More, John Gregson, Dinah Sheridan and Kay Kendall, were all wonderful, more often than not being pitchforked into an unscheduled scene after waiting for hours on the back of the open truck in rain and wind. Not a single shot was taken on the Brighton Road and, in purely academic terms, nothing matched photographically because of the wildly fluctuating light conditions. Yet, when the picture came to be shown, I received some of the best notices ever and not a voice was raised in protest about the geography. There must be a moral here somewhere, and it surely is that what matters most is the script.

"*Genevieve* became a big success at the box office and brought a well deserved reward to Henry Cornelius who, I am glad to say, was able to get his house and other possessions back, with interest. The Rank Organisation, at last aware of the film's potential, tried to buy out his interest, but he steadfastly refused all its offers. The first showing of the completed film was in the preview theatre at Technicolor. As the lights came up at the end, Earl St John, the American head of production, who had expressed little interest in the film during its making, rose to his feet and observed to Henry and the rest of us who made the movie, 'we may get a few car nuts to go along and see it in this country, but it won't do business anywhere else.' What a typical attitude from one who was supposed to be the arbiter of public taste; but then, what could you expect from someone with a name like that?"

CHAPTER
SEVEN

Members of the Veteran Car Club of Great Britain were very dubious about the whole idea of a film concerning their beloved Brighton run. They felt it might mock the rally, and so were initially loath to support the venture. Securing their interest and involvement, though, was of paramount importance, not least in order to bring them round enough to make their cars available for use in the film.

When the script was read, the club was mortified; "Impossible! You can't do this, and you can't do that." The proposed race back to London was the very antithesis of the club's ideals. Slowly, by tactful negotiation, a compromise was reached with assistance from the VCC chairman of the day, Evelyn Mawer. Mawer also got behind the sourcing of cars for crowd scenes when required, as well as the technical backup that might be needed to look after them. Making sure that a right and proper process was followed, the club issued its members with a memo headed *IMPORTANT ANNOUNCEMENT*. It explained that they had been asked to participate in a feature film woven around the Brighton run.

A special subcommittee had been set up to oversee arrangements, and to placate those who perhaps felt that the finished product may not have been in the best interests of the club.

No special costumes would be required, and members would be able to drive their own cars with passengers of their choice. Dates and times were issued for the scenes in question, along with the number of cars required. Those willing to partake with their cars were asked to complete the entry form attached, and to submit with it a good photograph of their vehicle. Those chosen would be at the discretion of the committee and the film company, whose joint decisions would be final.

From a lump sum of money – offered to the VCC by the Rank Organisation to cover organising costs – out of pocket expenses would be paid to individuals whose cars were chosen for the film, but who could not be there with them. It had to be borne in mind though, explained the committee, that each disbursement would mean less for the club's funds. In the end, almost 40 members and their cars made nearly 100 appearances, subjecting themselves to one confusing instruction after another, endless stopping and starting, back tracking, and moving forward again.

Opposite: The announcement to Veteran Car Club members, requesting them to provide their vehicles for 'a film based around the annual London to Brighton run.'

THE VETERAN CAR CLUB OF GREAT BRITAIN

IMPORTANT ANNOUNCEMENT

SPECIAL FILM EVENT - SEPTEMBER AND OCTOBER 1952

Our Club has been asked to participate in a First Feature Film in Technicolour, to be made in September and October by the Director of the very successful films "Passport to Pimlico" "Hue and Cry" and the "Galloping Major" etc., in which the story is woven around the BRIGHTON RUN.

A special Sub-Committee has been dealing with this for some time, and members can rest assured that all scenes etc., will be in the best traditions of the Club; no special costumes will be required and members will drive their own cars with their own passengers.

Veteran cars up to 1904 will be required for the following scenes, all of which will be made out-of-doors:-

1. On or about 15 cars, drivers and passengers in south London streets
   18.9.52 &   required for all day, start 8.30 a.m.
   19.9.52

2. On or about 35 cars, drivers and passengers required in Hyde Park at
   23.9.52   8.30 a.m. for filming start of "Brighton Run."

3. On or about 10 cars, drivers and passengers in south London streets
   20.9.52   and urban scenes required for all day, start 8.30 a.m.

4. On or about 15 cars, drivers and passengers required in BRIGHTON all day.
   5.10.52   start 8.30 a.m.

5. On or about A pool of about 15 cars, drivers and passengers (if possible)
   27,29,30.9.   to be available with 48 hours notice for use at various venues
   & 1,20.10.52   either Brighton Road, or road scenes adjacent to studios
                  (West London), start 8.30 a.m.

The film Company has offered a lump sum of money to our Club to cover all the organising expenses, and this has been accepted.

Will those members who are willing to attend with their car/s any or all of the above meetings, please complete and return the entry form appended below by RETURN OF POST and submit with their entry form a good photograph of their car/s, if available. Entries will be entirely by selection, and the decisions of the special Committee and the Film Company will be final.

From the sum of money paid to the Club, out-of-pocket expenses may be paid to those who could not otherwise attend, but it must be borne in mind that every disbursement means less for the Club funds.

. . . .

ENTRY FORM   (BLOCK CAPITALS PLEASE)

NAME & ADDRESS OF ENTRANT. . . . .
& TELEPHONE NO:. . . . .

MAKE OF CAR . . . . .YEAR . . . .HP . . . .BODY . . . .

COLOUR SCHEME . . . . NO. OF SEATS . . V.C.C. CLUB NO. . . . .

NO. OF PASSENGERS . . . . . MY CAR WILL BE AVAILABLE FOR 1 2 3 4 5
                                        (strike out as necessary)

I shall not require any expenses.
I shall require about   for various.

If my car is selected for this,
indemnified the Veteran Car Club
and their representatives only

Firstly, two cars had to be located as the mechanical stars. Despite the decidedly French name given to the four-wheeled leading player, it was a British car that Cornelius had a preference for in both cases; a Wolseley, or perhaps a Humber, for Genevieve, and a Lanchester for her rival. A Lanchester, though, was considered too complicated to drive – even if it could be found – and anyway, it didn't have a bonnet. In William Rose's first draft of the *Genevieve* screenplay – dated July 22nd 1952 – his star car was referred to as a 1903 De Dion Bouton, and was paired up with a 1904 7hp Oldsmobile runabout as its competitor. Curiously, like the Lanchester it also didn't have a bonnet. By the time the final shooting script was ready, complete with storyboard sketches for each scene, the De Dion and Oldsmobile were still very much part of the scenario. Given that filming got under way on or about September 14th, it would seem quite possible that the decision to use the Darracq and the Spyker was a late one. Both starring vehicles would be required for a three-month shooting schedule, while 35 veterans were needed for the Hyde Park departure scenes – 10 here, 15 there – and at least 20 for the arrival scenes in Brighton.

While Rose's script talked of the two main cars as though they had already been found, the fact remained that no one was prepared to subject their veterans to three months of wear and tear in the hands of total strangers. It was obviously a sticking point, and one not properly solved until a member of the film crew happened to pass by the Ford Motor showrooms of Norman Reeves in Uxbridge High Street, not far from Pinewood Studios in Buckinghamshire. Norman Reeves, for his own interest, had been completing the restoration of a 1904 Darracq that was just visible though the showroom window. After an

Behind Genevieve's steering wheel is Norman Reeves' restorer Charlie Cadby who stood in at times for John Gregson during filming. Henry Cornelius is on the motorbike.

initial approach from the studio, Reeves agreed to lend his Darracq to the production, not in any way anticipating the international celebrity status the car would eventually attract. He insisted, however, that Charlie Cadby – one of his own mechanics, who had been responsible for much of the Darracq's restoration – should be on hand to service the car during the shooting schedule.

Another veteran owner, taxi driver Frank Reece, offered his Spyker. The model was the only Dutch-made car in the club, which would ultimately prove to be the perfect adversary to Genevieve.

All that was needed now were the human stars. Of the four selected, three were up and coming performers, whilst the fourth – Dinah Sheridan – was already well established. She had recently starred in *Where No Vultures Fly*, filmed in Kenya, and was chosen for the 1951 Royal Command Performance.

Returning home from the studios one day, where she was filming the World War Two story *Appointment in London* with Dirk Bogarde, Dinah opened her mail and found three scripts to read. Two of the roles, she felt, might be hers if she wanted them, while *Genevieve* – obviously the pick of the trio – would no doubt be much more competitively sought after. Landing the role

of Wendy McKim seemed too much to hope for, particularly when Claire Bloom had been rumoured as first choice. Talking it over with Dirk Bogarde, who had been offered Alan McKim's role and turned it down, he told her to "go for it, it's really you."

Henry Cornelius summoned Dinah to a lunch in a restaurant in Mayfair, London. Over the meal, he deflated her somewhat by saying, "Of course, you realise you are far too old for the part." She was 31 at the time. "Well that's it," she thought, "I've blown it, but I'll enjoy the free lunch."

Cornelius's wife Marjory was also at that luncheon. She would later recall, "What Dinah didn't know, and perhaps has never known, was that when she got up to go to the cloakroom, one of a group of city gentlemen sitting at a nearby table was heard to comment, as she passed by, 'My godfathers, there's a beautiful creature if ever I saw one.' That remark might just about have made up my husband's mind."

CHAPTER
EIGHT

Dinah was cast as Wendy McKim, the wife to Alan, as portrayed by John Gregson. Alan was a serious young barrister, whose pride and joy was his family's Darracq, Genevieve, which he had inherited.

John Gregson – the unsmiling Scot, as he was known – had appeared in limited secondary roles in several major British movies of the time. His manner was deemed by Cornelius to be a perfect contrast, and appropriately so, to the caddish, roguish advertising executive Ambrose Claverhouse. Ambrose had been a best friend to Alan and Wendy for years, and had even introduced them. Unmarried himself, he took a different girl with him on the run to Brighton each year. He obviously adored the stunningly pretty Wendy, and openly admitted he should have married her himself, obviously peeving Alan. In all, Ambrose was a likeable blowhard. He maintained that his Spyker could beat Genevieve any day, anywhere; this was a claim which didn't always make for harmony between the two male mates.

Kenneth More had, at this time, been on the verge of abandoning his acting career due to lack of work. Luckily, however, he landed a plumb role in Terrance Rattigan's play *The Deep Blue Sea*. Henry Cornelius saw the play during the time he was casting for *Genevieve*, and

thought More to be brilliant. More's subsequent portrayal of Ambrose Claverhouse rocketed him to international stardom.

His perfect foil and girlfriend in *Genevieve* was Kay Kendall, found after Cornelius had seen her in the film *London Town*. The film itself was a disaster, but Kendall's performance was memorable. She possessed the glamorous, uninhibited vivaciousness needed to carry off the character, in particular the tiddly trumpet playing scene at the dinner dance, held in Brighton for rally contestants after the day's run down from London.

Filming took place out of sequence over the last three months of 1952. The first scene to go before the cameras was of Wendy finding a chicken drumstick in her picnic hamper and feeding it to Alan as he lay under Genevieve, attempting to work out why a noise in the motor had heralded an unscheduled stop on the way to Brighton. In reality, both the Darracq and the Spyker ran faultlessly as they fulfilled their respective responsibilities at the behest of

Continued page 50

Opposite and overleaf: Two Marjory Cornelius costume designs, as worn by Dinah Sheridan playing Wendy McKim in Genevieve.

WENDY
Car rally to Brighton - first half
-

Blue/grey dress
Edwardian motoring hat
High heeled shoes

An original, incorrectly oil-coloured, promotional 'still.' The scene depicted was the first to go before the cameras as filming Genevieve got under way.

JOHN GREGSON • DINAH SHERIDAN

IN

GENEVIEVE

COLOUR BY TECHNICOLOR

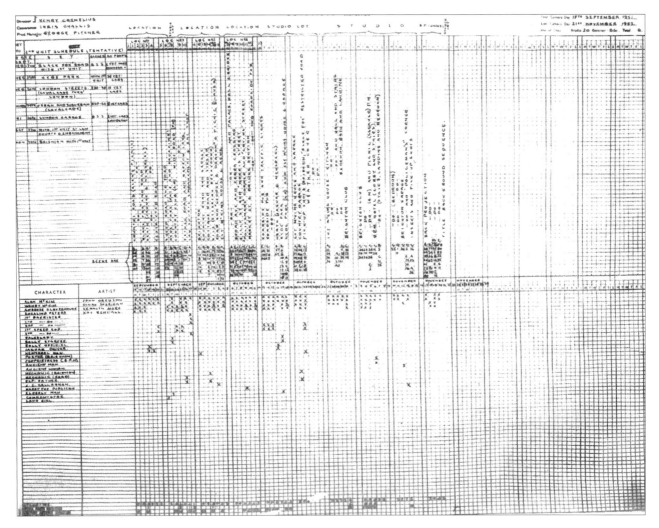

The 1952 filming schedule for Genevieve.

producer Henry Cornelius. At the time, John Gregson didn't actually have a driver's licence; something of a myth has been bandied around over the years that he couldn't even drive. He could – and did – drive himself to the studios, but had not taken his test. Despite this, manhandling the Darracq was indeed an issue for John. It worried him, and irritated a stomach ulcer he was already nursing. To help ease the discomfort, he surreptitiously placed a glass of milk on Genevieve's floor to guzzle down whenever

he could, hoping it would assist in relieving the symptoms.

There were a few near misses during filming. One particular incident with a bus was never forgotten, after it apparently just appeared from nowhere. As Dinah Sheridan recalls, "A case of panic was my lot each morning; by night-time, a wreck." Intense cold didn't help much either; the weather was bitter. Dirk Bogarde had given Dinah a mohair rug after completing their film together, which she used over her knees in Genevieve

Between scenes, Dinah Sheridan puts a hot water bottle under a blanket on her knee.

to hide hot water bottles! The production team supplied brandy first thing in the mornings to obscure the blue look of the actors' faces, in case the cameras should pick it up. On the days when clouds threatened, mobile high-powered generators and two dozen arc lamps were trundled around the countryside to provide artificial sun.

The 'action,' however, hardly visited the traditional London to Brighton road. The majority of the outdoor scenes 'en route' were filmed miles away near Pinewood Studios in Buckinghamshire. Local motorists were completely bewildered; signs announcing 'Brighton: 10 miles' suddenly sprang up in quiet country roads, whilst others in

dead-end lanes purported to point to London 25 miles away. In fact, the story goes that a country police officer awoke one morning to find his front garden had sprouted a pole, bearing a placard that read 'Cattle Crossing Beware!'

The coffee-spilling scene was filmed outside Moor Park golf course in Hertfordshire. Windsor Great Park also made a guest appearance, as did the Jolly Woodman pub at Burnham Beeches in Buckinghamshire.

The Cornelius children were roped in for the zebra crossing hold-up scene, filmed in the Old Kent Road. Their daughter took some convincing to wear scruffy clothes for filming, worried

Continued page 56

The famous coffee-spilling scene, set en route to Brighton but filmed outside the Moor Park golf course in Hertfordshire.

The McKims alongside the Spyker's owner Ambrose Claverhouse (Kenneth More), his current girlfriend Rosalind Peters (Kay Kendall), and her hound Suzie. (Photo by ITV/REX/Shutterstock)

Marjory and Henry Cornelius' daughter plays her part on a zebra crossing, during the race from Brighton back to London's Westminster bridge.

The zebra crossing scene from a different angle.

Cameras roll alongside the Serpentine in London's Hyde Park as the McKims line up in Genevieve to start for Brighton.

what her friends might think, while the endless ice creams required for each retake resulted in putting her off them entirely for a long time afterwards.

All outside scenes involving cars en masse were completed by the end of October. Whiling away breaks on location, Dinah Sheridan would often be getting on with her knitting. Kay Kendall had struck up an off-screen friendship with her on-screen pet, a St Bernard dog called Suzie. The dog had undergone a sex change from William Rose's first draft of the script, where it was referred to as

*BBC interviewer Leslie Mitchell, playing himself, has a word with Alan and Wendy
as they wait for the departure call from Hyde Park.*

Simon. Kenneth More, meanwhile, had formed an enthusiast's attachment to the yellow Dutch Spyker, whilst John Gregson spent his free time adding to his knowledge of driving a less-than-modern motor car. When it leaked out later that he had no licence at the outset of filming, some VCC owners felt righteously justified in not making their cars available for use before the cameras.

It was found, though, that the 35 cars and drivers organised by the VCC for the departure scenes in Hyde Park and the arrival in Brighton, plus

Continued page 60

Storyboard details for the opening title sequences of the film Genevieve, from Rose's revised screenplay. Owing to budget restraints they were never used.

After the J. Arthur Rank gong -

   DISSOLVE:

A flag, filling the screen is fluttering in the
wind.

CAMERA tracks back to reveal it is in the hands of a
footman dressed in period costume, preceding a Victorian
automobile.

The driver and his lady passenger resplendent in Victorian
dress, are concentrating on the dangerous task of steering
their vehicle along the Queen's Highway - at the phenomenal
speed of 5 m.p.h.

As we PAN with the car and CAMERA holds it in back view,
an enormous cloud of white smoke issues from the exhaust,
billowing up until it blots out the entire screen.

Over a continuous background of swirling smoke we superimpose
the CREDIT TITLES.

At the end of the credit titles:

               FOREWORD

          For their patient co-operation the
     makers of this film express their thanks to
     the Officers and Members of the Veteran Car
     Club of Great Britain.

          Any resemblance between the characters
     in our story and any actual Members of the
     Club is emphatically denied --- by the Club.

As the foreword fades and the smoke behind it starts
thinning out, gradually the contours of the first scene of
the film begin to emerge:

Production instructions describing storyboard sketches for Genevieve's opening title sequences.

Filming Genevieve's opening Law Court scenes in London's Strand. (Photo by ITV/REX/Shutterstock)

a few hundred onlookers, hardly did justice to the real event. As a result, footage from the genuine 1952 London to Brighton run was woven into the final production for the sake of authenticity.

Right from the outset, the making of *Genevieve* was bedevilled by substantial financial restraints. This had a considerable effect on the finished product, with scenes included in the screenplay, that would have further enhanced the film, being pared down or – in some cases – cut out completely. For example, had this not been the case, the opening scenes would have had quite a different format.

According to the screenplay, following the image of the J Arthur Rank gong dissolving,

The much-pared-down title introduction of the finished film Genevieve.

which traditionally announced its films of the 1950s, a flag would have appeared filling the screen as it fluttered in the breeze. The camera would track back to reveal the flag to be in the hands of a footman dressed in period costume, preceding a veteran car. The driver and his female passenger, both in clothing of the era, are seen concentrating on steering their pride and joy along at the breathtaking speed of 5mph. As it passes, the camera holds the vehicle in back view. An enormous cloud of white smoke blows out from the exhaust, billowing up until it blots out the whole screen. Over a continuous background of swirling smoke the credit titles are superimposed.

We then see the character of barrister Alan McKim running from the Law Courts in The Strand, not to a Darracq called Genevieve parked outside in the Aldwych (as in the film), but to a De Dion Bouton along the Embankment with 'Genevieve' embossed on its side. The action then moves to a chic-looking Mayfair hat shop. Genevieve is heard approaching, her arrival reflected in the shop window. Alan is shown going in and being greeted by a sales lady who appears to be expecting him. A purchasing scene follows before Alan departs with a hat box and motors home to his and Wendy's mews cottage.

Driving into the garage is, of course, what we see in the released film, as though he has gone there directly from the Law Courts. The introduction scenes, as described, would arguably have been a more entertaining beginning than the simplified version adopted for the finished film.

CHAPTER
NINE

Frustrations pertaining to exterior work scored some memorable, albeit totally unscripted, scenes. While they were giggled at later by the cast, the frustration at the time meant that they weren't seen as so funny then. Henry Cornelius was a stickler for getting it right, and on one occasion, in the pouring rain, he requested More and Kendall to drive toward the camera repeatedly until he was satisfied. Soaked and miserable, Kay Kendall suddenly snapped. She jumped down from the passenger seat of the Spyker, grabbed a huge umbrella, housed in a wicker holder on the side of the car, and rushed over to Cornelius, who had been directing from the roadside. Bashing him time and time again around the head, she screamed, "You rotten little bastard; how dare you do this to us in these foul stinking conditions!"

Henry's wife Marjory – whose costume designs for the film drew much praise from fashion commentators of the day – had further memories of the mercurial Kay Kendall, which she shared with me at her Hampshire home in 1993:

"I arrived at Kay's flat one morning, to discuss her fittings. Wrapped only in a towel, she opened the front door exclaiming that she had sent all her clothes to the dry cleaners, and her underwear to the laundry but that I should come in anyway and have some champagne. Kay dispensed with the towel and sat there without a stitch on while we discussed what was needed and drank our bubbly."

Once, while on location and between takes, cast and crew rushed into a pub for warmth and a drink. Kay stood too close to an electric fire and set the back of her skirt alight, which was subsequently ruined. Marjory had to dash up to

An off-camera shot showing cast, crew, and curious onlookers, waiting for the coffee pouring scene to be filmed.

A sozzled Rosalind (Kay Kendall) plays her trumpet solo at the Brighton dinner dance.
(Photo by ITV/REX/Shutterstock)

London, to Victor Stiebel who made the costumes, and ask for some more cloth. "But only yesterday," he replied, "did I send the remainder to the sale rooms." Marjory hastened to the sale rooms, only to find a woman telling the assistant "I'll have this, thank you." "Oh no you won't," cried Marjory, and – whipping away the required piece – went back to the set to patch Kay's garment.

In the much-remembered trumpet playing scene, the postwar fabric of Kay's voluptuous black evening gown kept falling out of shape. Keeping it figure hugging, as it was intended to be, meant securing it with a safety pin on the back. Kay was instructed to do the scene facing the camera and not to move in either direction, let alone turn around. The actress suffered something of a nervous attack as she was about to play her on-screen solo. The script called for her, in a state of happy inebriation, to enquire of her fellow characters – Alan, Wendy and Ambrose – if they would like to hear her play the trumpet. In error, Kay said 'plumpet.' Director Henry Cornelius thought it funny enough to leave in, but didn't live long enough to enjoy an amusing footnote regarding the scene's authenticity, as later relayed to me by his widow.

Some years later, Kenneth More was in America watching a show where a tough-looking native demonstrated his ability to wrestle with an alligator. He apparently spotted More looking on, and later enquired of him in a beautifully-spoken voice if in fact it was really Kay Kendall playing the trumpet in *Genevieve*.

When filming moved into the studio for the interior scenes, a negative atmosphere hung in the air. The Rank Organisation frankly had little faith in their veteran car project, and being acknowledged as a low-budget affair destined to go nowhere – or so it was considered – had started to affect the cast's morale.

John Gregson and Kay Kendall were far from cheerful, the latter desperately wanting to be released from her contract. However, being half way through production, it just wasn't possible.

A big-budget Disney film was in progress at Pinewood at the time, using practically all the available studio floor space. The *Genevieve* interior shots were, as a result, squeezed into whatever space was left. Then, seven eighths of the way through the film, the company ran out of money. The whole thing was well over budget by this point, due to Cornelius liking to repeat each shot until he got one he was satisfied with. He had, however, taken out an insurance policy against such a contingency and was paid £20,000, a large lump sum for

those days. The insurance company was far from pleased, and despatched its scouts to Pinewood to implement cost-cutting exercises, such as switching off any lights that were not required.

One of the most enchanting aspects of the film *Genevieve* is its theme music. This was composed and played by the internationally renowned harmonica player Larry Adler, who – although American born – had lived in England since 1949. Larry was playing the piano one night at a party when a member of the Rank publicity team (who was listening) asked the name of the tune that was leaping off the ivories. "It's nothing," came the reply, "I'm making it up." Such was the impression it made, that the performance was conveyed to Henry Cornelius; his composer may well have been found.

Cornelius was duly swayed, and asked Larry to write the *Genevieve* music score. "I couldn't possibly, I've never written a film melody in my life," he replied. In fact, he had never actually written anything. Larry found it quite a task to convince the producer that he wasn't the man for the job.

At best, Larry had only nine months of study in music composition to his name. If he hadn't had even that small amount of tuition, he claims today that he could not have done the *Genevieve* score; the idea frightened him to death.

About this time, he found himself in New York. He was staying with a friend on Long Island who had ordered a new Cadillac car, and Larry was asked if he would collect it from the Manhattan

*Opposite: Original sheet music
for the Genevieve Waltz.*

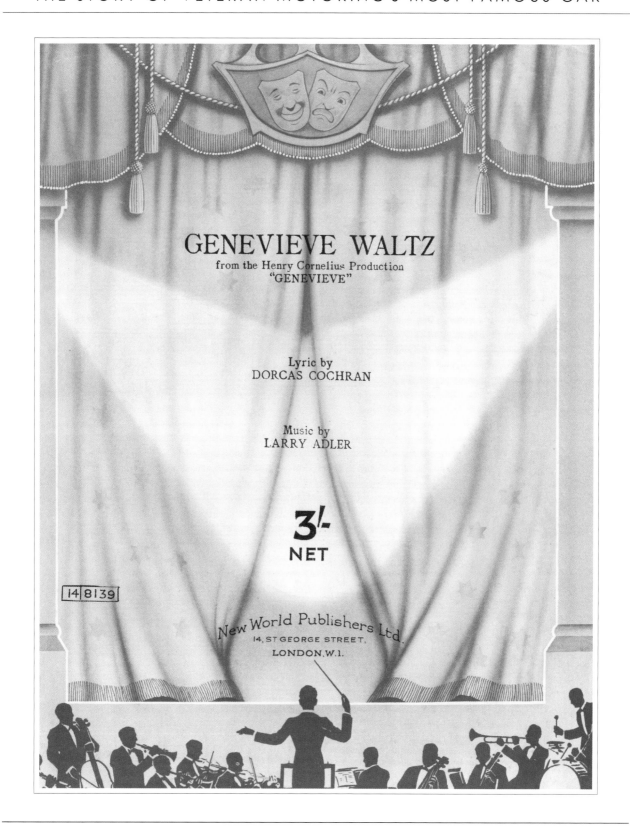

showroom. While driving it back, he became trapped in a Fifth Avenue traffic jam. He pulled over to the kerb, the idea for a tune suddenly springing into his mind. Taking out a piece of manuscript paper (which he always carried) from his wallet, he wrote down the first eight bars of *Genevieve*. However, it would take another two months to write the next eight bars.

Although under way with his arrangement, Larry considered his efforts lousy to such a degree whereby the already-finished film could be ruined with it. Nevertheless, the rest is musical history! He has since written another 12 movie music scores, but Henry Cornelius remains the only producer who wanted to hear the music as it was being composed, rather than afterward.

CHAPTER
TEN

Having accepted the *Genevieve* assignment, Larry Adler was embarrassed to find the news announced to all and sundry at a party he attended at Les Ambassador, the exclusive London Club off Park Lane. Another of the guests happened to be the head of United Artists who, Larry understood, called Rank and said if Larry Adler's music was in *Genevieve*, the film would not get an American release; at the time, Larry was blacklisted in the States for his left wing political views. Cornelius rang Larry and let him know that he'd been asked to fire him, but that this was the last thing that needed to be done.

With Larry continuing with the project, his agent then took over. There had been no signed contract by this point, only a verbal agreement. Originally the agent had, on Larry's behalf, asked for a fee of £750 for him to write the score. Rank responded with, "No, too much." £500: still too much. At the end of the day, all that was on offer was a 2.5 per cent share of the film's returns. The agent's subsequent advice to his client was to scrub it; the film's a fizzer, a quota picture, and will never recoup its costs.

Contrary to this and all other advice, Larry decided to take a gamble on the film. It was the first motion picture music score he'd been asked to do, and what if – against the odds – it was a success? What then?

Of course, as we know now, it was. Larry Adler never failed to admit that the money he made from *Genevieve* had educated his children in private schools; the royalty cheques just kept rolling in. Relating this story one day to Dinah Sheridan, she rounded on him saying, "Larry, I wish you hadn't told me about that; we all got a flat fee of £3,500 and had to get on with it."

Larry wasn't fired in the end; instead, he had to grant the studio the right to include him – or not – on the film's billing. So, for the English print of the film, he was given due credit for the music composition and the playing of it.

Six weeks later, before *Genevieve* opened in New York, the exhibitors asked that Larry's name be removed for the American release. In order to comply, a whole new set of credits had to be made, and when the film finally opened in New York there was simply no composer listed. Then, in one of those instances of delicious irony – as Larry himself has noted – the music was nominated for an Oscar, with no composer! When the Rank Organisation was asked who wrote the music, they gave the name of Muir Mathieson, who had conducted the orchestra. He never wrote a note.

Two years later, Larry and Muir met at a function. Larry asked him, "How could you possibly accept the nomination for *Genevieve*?"

Harmonica player Larry Adler, conductor Muir Mathieson, and film producer Henry Cornelius, working on Genevieve's Oscar-nominated music score.

Muir replied, "Well, I thought it was for services to British music!"

Not until 1991 was the situation remedied for once and for all, when Adler was playing in a concert at the Hollywood Bowl in Los Angeles. A young man there, who had worked at the Hollywood Academy, approached Larry and said he could recall seeing a British print of *Genevieve* with the music credit to Larry Adler on it. The informant approached the Academy with his findings, and kept at them until they sent Adler a nomination certificate as the composer for the *Genevieve* melody; nearly 40 years late!

The premiere of *Genevieve* at London's Leicester Square cinema in May 1953 – for which all Veteran Car Club participants received double tickets – was something of a moral booster for all involved in its production. This was owing to the positive public reaction in an earlier trial screening, in the suburb of Camden Town. As if to placate any club members who may have their noses put out of joint by what the screen would show them,

a softener – with a tongue in cheek slant – was added to the movie's introduction:

"For their patient co-operation, the makers of this film express their thanks to the officers and members of the Veteran Car Club of Great Britain. Any resemblance between the deportment of the characters and any club members is emphatically denied – by the club."

Henry Cornelius couldn't feel confident about cinemagoers' acceptance of the film he had put his life on the line for, and being offered an honorary membership of the VCC wasn't going to convince him either. He did, though, tentatively observe to his wife at the end of this first screening, "It's going

Continued page 73

Opposite: A reproduction of a promotional letter from The Rank Organisation to the editor of the VCC's Veteran Car Gazette announcing Genevieve's West End premiere.

J. ARTHUR RANK ORGANIZATION LTD

38 SOUTH STREET W1
Telegrams: JAROFILM AUDLEY LONDON
Telephone: MAYFAIR 7454

14th May 1953

The Editor,
The Veteran Car Gazette,
Veteran Car Club of Great Britain,
46 North Street,
London W1

Dear Sir,

We thought you might be interested in the enclosed still from our new production, "Genevieve" which will have its premieres in the West End next month.

"Genevieve," Pinewood Studio's new comedy-of-cars, tells the story of two veteran car addicts "who, in the jet age, continue to drive about in mechanical boneshakers that were old-fashioned before Orville Wright took to flying the Kitty Hawk."

The idea is an unusual one and we thought you might find this still amusing. We have also englosed a coverage story of "Genevieve."

If you should decide to use the picture, we should very much appreciate a credit to the film.

Sincerely,

Jack Atack.

Directors: J ARTHUR RANK J.P. (Chairman) JOHN DAVIS (Managing Director)
K.N. HARGREAVES ⎱ Joint Assistant
K. WINCKLES ⎰ Managing Directors
G.I. WOODHAM-SMITH

The cast and crew of Genevieve.

The McKims damp and despondent on the road to Brighton. (Photo by ITV/REX/Shutterstock)

to make people laugh." Few involved in the making of the film were game enough to prophesy the public's reaction. Chief executives at Rank had seen the film and couldn't get excited about it. Even the publicity was as thin on the ground as had been the money to finance the low-budget production in the first place. Somehow, however, and as sure as night follows day, film fans began warming to the theme. Word of mouth spread with astonishing results, and *Genevieve* became an unmitigated success, being named Best British Film for 1953. The road to immortality had been embarked upon; in the documented history of the Rank Organisation's Pinewood Studios, where the film was made, it is stated that the film was one of the most successful motion pictures ever produced there. Once out on general release, *Genevieve* played in cinemas around the world, sometimes for weeks and months at a time.

"The pleasures of laughter; I listened to those waves of gaiety that swept over the room, and when the show was finished I saw its freshness reflected in the faces of the audience." So wrote the film critic of *Le Figaro* when *Genevieve* opened at the Paris Cinema in the Champs-Élysées, later breaking all records. Many more were smashed in Brussels and Amsterdam. At the Sutton Cinema in New York, an all time record was taken.

Genevieve was Britain's representative at Brazil's São Paulo film festival, whilst in Australia, Melbourne's Odeon Theatre shook with laughter each night during a lengthy run of unprecedented proportions.

Needless to say, the Veteran Car Club of Great Britain prospered handsomely overnight, while old car clubs around the globe sprang up in the most unlikely places.

Continued page 76

Announcing a Genevieve screening in Paris.

Promoting Genevieve's release in Picturegoer magazine.

2 for the lau

GENEVIEVE

There was a time when Ealing was regarded as the home of British film comedy. Things have changed. It seems they're all on the laughter road now. And here's one picture that starts out in top gear and stays the course that way. It spotlights the lighter side of the Veteran Car Club's annual London to Brighton rally, a real day out for the proud owners of old crocks—although I doubt that the real thing ever packs so many mishaps as this did: but the film is no mishap

LAWYER
son) is v
Genevieve
Sheridan),
keen on t

interview Alan at the start-ing point comes Leslie Mitchell of the B.B.C. Alan tells the listeners he's carry-ing on a family tradition.

For both
along the
get to Bri
a merry
how the

ghter road

by JOHN FITZGERALD
The man who discussed films on TV
talks about two British comedies
that go out on the rounds next week

an McKim (John Greg-
fond of his old crock,
His wife, Wendy (Dinah
wever, is not nearly so
old girl." It's time for

the Brighton Rally, and Ambrose
Claverhouse (Kenneth More) plans to
combine his favourite pastimes on the
jaunt. One is his old car: the other is
his new girl, Rosalind (Kay Kendall).

The old crocks set out from Hyde
Park. There are hundreds of venerable vehicles with gleaming paint,
burnished brass and newly trimmed
lamp-wicks at the start. And to

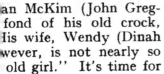

couples there's trouble
e. But they eventually
n. At the party there,
salind shows the band
npet should be played.

There's a reaction—she passes out.
But the fun goes on. Alan and
Ambrose wager £100 on a race back
to town—and Alan is booked by the
police for driving at fifty. Ambrose

has trouble too. His car sticks in a
ford. He makes Rosalind push it out of
the water. Rosalind is getting rather
tired of veteran cars by now. But
I don't think you'll get travel-tired.

Norman Reeves driving John Gregson up the Long Walk to Windsor Castle during the 1953 Coronation Rally.

Only a couple of weeks after the film's premiere showing, Genevieve made her first public guest appearance on June 7th, in the Veteran Car Club's Coronation Rally at Windsor, which attracted a record 220 entrants. With the Darracq's New Zealand ties still some way into the future, it is interesting to note that Kiwi Andrew "Andy" Anderson – later a huge influence in the Vintage Car Club of New Zealand – was on hand to sell programmes. Almost 15 years later, as National President of the club, Andy took an interest in a shortish biographical essay that I, as a budding teenage author, proposed to write on Genevieve. He prompted his wife Mollie, then editor of the club's monthly journal *Beaded Wheels*, to publish it. This became my first piece

Continued page 80

Promoting Genevieve's release in a film magazine of the day.

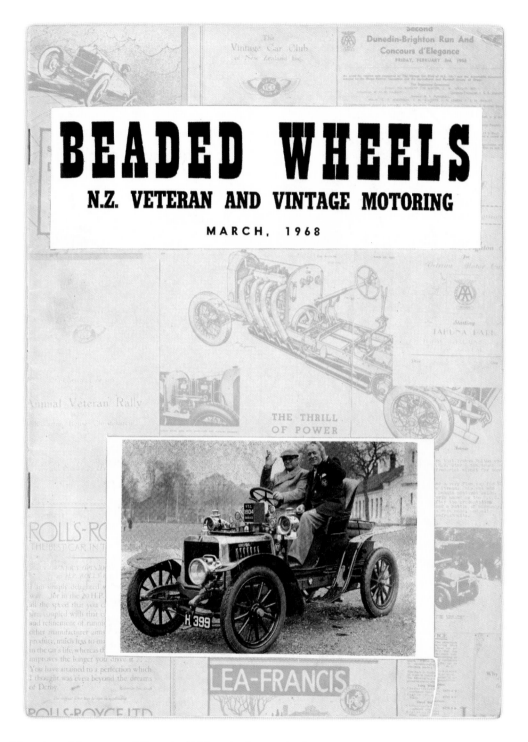

The March 1968 cover of Beaded Wheels, journal of the Vintage Car Club of New Zealand, featuring Norman Reeves and passenger in Genevieve.

An original Genevieve cinema poster.

A post-film shot – at the Place de la Concorde in Paris – of Norman Reeves with his wife in Genevieve, plus Frank Reece with his wife and two friends in the Spyker.

*Opposite: A page from Luxemberg's
1955 automobile booklet.*

'. . . as much a part of the British scene as
the Tower of London or Lord's cricket ground.'

WHO would have thought that a
film about so English an eccentricity as a veteran car rally would have
cosmopolitan appeal? Certainly Pinewood Studios did—and GENEVIEVE has

The Amazing Adventures of GENEVIEVE

WORLD TOUR

'The pleasures of laughter ! I listened to those
waves of gaiety that swept over the room ; and
when the show was finished I saw its freshness
reflected in the faces of the audience.' So wrote
the film critic of *Le Figaro* when GENEVIEVE
opened at the Paris Cinema in the Champs-
Elysées later to smash all house records.
More records were broken in Brussels and
Amsterdam. In Zurich and Stockholm
GENEVIEVE played to capacity houses.
On the other side of the Atlantic, too,
it has won laurels — acclaimed right
across Canada ; with an all-time record
at the Sutton Cinema in New York; as
British representative at Brazil's Sao
Paulo Film Festival.
In Melbourne, on June 29th last year,
GENEVIEVE smashed all house records
at the Odeon Cinema.

chugged a long, long way since she
first took the London-to-Brighton
road. No sleek limousine or high-powered racing car has ever equalled the
success of this lovable veteran; nor
earned so many valuable prizes in so
many countries. For this gay comedy
is winning pounds and pesetas, kroner
and guilders, francs and escudos—
dollars too. What's more, it's an ex-
port which millions have enjoyed at
home.

EXPORT DRIVE

*This film is only one illustration of the remarkable
recovery of British films during the last few years—
of the success that they are now enjoying overseas.
(Last year 50% of the Rank Group's film earnings
came from abroad.) It's good to know that this
section of the British Film Industry is once more
in top gear.*

THE J. ARTHUR RANK ORGANISATION LIMITED

*Rank Organisation PR material
for Genevieve, 1953.*

to appear in print, spearheading an interest in
freelance writing that has never diminished. Back
to Genevieve's memorable June appearance,
and also on hand was the former Governor
General of New Zealand, Lieutenant General
Lord Freyberg VC. As Deputy Constable and
Lieutenant Governor of the Royal Borough of
Windsor, Lord Freyberg welcomed competitors
and crew to the castle's Long Walk.

MANDAG 13. MAI 1957

GENEVIEVE OG 45 ANDRE VETERANER INNTAR OSLO

Imponerende mønstring av veteran-biler på Festningsplassen i Oslo

Den stolte Genevieve — som gikk til filmen — kjører ut i Oslo-trafikken med sin stolte eier

*A Norwegian newspaper account
of Genevieve in Oslo.*

auto route

Pour Geneviève

Connaissez-vous Geneviève, Madame?
Et vous, Monsieur?

Non...

Dommage!

Si vous connaissiez Geneviève, il serait superflu de vous expliquer pourquoi nous lui dédions le premier numéro d'AUTOROUTE.

Permettez-nous donc de vous la présenter: sa photo est sous vos yeux.

Oui, c'est elle, la Darracq 1904, l'héroïne du film que vous n'avez pas vu.

Vous n'avez vraiment pas de chance. Vous qui aimez votre voiture au point de lui avoir donné un nom: Colette, parce que vous l'avez achetée le 6 mars, son jour de fête, — vous auriez dû voir ce film délicieux, l'histoire d'amour d'Alan McKim qui ne pouvait se séparer de la Darracq de son grand-père et dont le cœur follement épris de mécanique balançait entre sa Geneviève cinquantenaire et sa jolie jeune femme Wendy.

Vous souriez, Madame. L'histoire vous rappelle un autre mari qui, sans être Anglais ni membre d'un « Club des vieux tacots », redevient gamin comme Alan McKim, quand il est aux petits soins avec sa voiture sport 1954.

Puisque vous souriez, vous avez déjà compris qu'en choisissant Geneviève comme marraine, nous dédions AUTO-ROUTE à tous les automobilistes pour qui l'auto n'est pas un moyen de transport comme les autres, mais une chose animée, qu'on aime pour elle-même et pour les plaisirs qu'elle vous donne.

Mais nous avons une deuxième raison pour placer notre revue sous le charmant patronage de Geneviève, la Darracq 1904.

Les hommes qui fondèrent notre Club et qui veillent encore sur ses destinées ont connu Geneviève. Elle fut le grand amour de leurs vingt ans, et c'est cet amour qui donna naissance à tous les Automobile Clubs. C'est à eux, les pionniers de la première heure, que l'automobile doit son essor prestigieux.

Qu'ils trouvent ici, en guise de préface à cette revue, l'expression de notre gratitude et notre engagement à servir la cause de l'automobile avec la même passion qu'ils éprouvèrent il y a cinquante ans pour Geneviève.

Au nom de Geneviève, nous souhaitons à tous nos membres un joyeux Noël et une heureuse année 1955.

3

Before that significant year was out, the little French two-seater was well and truly entrenched as a crowd pleaser. Nowhere, at that point, was this more apparent than the 1953 London to Brighton run, held in appalling weather on Sunday November 2nd. Despite the rain, huge crowds turned out to see, in reality, the mechanical star of what was becoming one of the most popular movies of all time. Dutch rally driver 'Maus' Gatsonides, winner of the year's Monte Carlo Rally, drove Genevieve from Hyde Park to the finishing line on Brighton's Madeira Drive.

Norman Reeves never anticipated such an outcome, nor the resulting – seemingly incessant – demands for his Darracq's appearance at fetes, rallies, fundraisers, and openings throughout the British Isles. The success or failure of any number of European rallies also suddenly depended on Genevieve being there. She had become the mascot of the veteran car movement worldwide.

Apart from the Brighton runs before and after Annie's reincarnation as Genevieve (seven altogether, between 1950 and 1957), Reeves drove his Darracq in a variety of events. These included putting her through her paces on the Silverstone and Goodwood race tracks, the Coronation Rally of 1953 (in which actor John Gregson, who drove the car to movie stardom, travelled as a passenger), the 1954 Dutch Rally, and others in Luxembourg, Germany, and Norway. "She has a fine complexion, covered with badges and honours," her proud owner would say, "we are attaching them on the inner side of the dash now, because there is no room left on the front."

In 1957, the late George Gilltrap Snr – a Rootes Group dealer and old car fanatic from Rotorua in the North Island of New Zealand – had embarked on a three-month world tour to study vintage car museums, with the idea of opening one of his own.

George arrived in New Zealand as a youngster in 1924, coming from Ireland with his family, which included seven brothers and two sisters. A year later, aged 13, he was working as a teamster on the sunny, wide open Canterbury wheat fields of the South Island, taking his turn driving a bullock team hauling logs. Anything that could be pushed, pulled, or driven fascinated him. Two years later, he had scratched together enough money to buy the cheapest car then available. During the following years he went through as many motorcars as possible within his limited budget, none being older than 1914. In his spare time, he learnt how to handle a farm tractor, and soon became a very successful demonstrator of the machines in New Zealand's North Island.

During World War Two, George served overseas in an airfield construction unit. Returning home, he turned his hand to contracting and operating heavy machinery on farm and road developments in the bush around Rotorua. In due course he established the largest war surplus

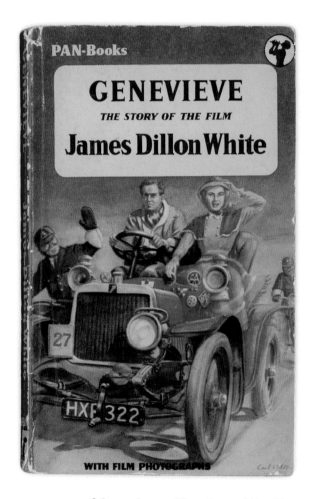

1955 cover of Genevieve – The story of the film, by James Dillon White, with a red Darracq! (Courtesy Pan Books)

disposal business in New Zealand and, in 1952, chartered a ship to bring back 300 tons of Jeeps and other equipment from the, then Dutch, New Guinea jungles.

Ultimately, George Gilltrap's interest in things mechanical extended to all vehicles. The first collectible car he purchased, an old Stanley Steamer discovered in 1939, was the start of what later became his museum collection. From time to time, as people heard of his interest, he was tipped off with information about old cars which he might be able to buy. When he saw the film *Genevieve*, his imagination was truly fired. Not only did he paint the name on the bonnet of an elderly Cadillac stored in his garage, but also decided – in 1954, with a certain amount of entrepreneurial flair – to display what old timers he then owned by setting up a museum attached to his Rotorua motoring business. As the Rootes dealership prospered, more and more old cars were found to add to his collection.

Continued page 87

1904 Darracq Wade beer mug made in Ireland, authenticated by the VCC of GB.

45:1 scale Matchbox 1904 Spyker from 'The Models of Yesteryear' collection.

A period advertisement capitalising on Genevieve's public appeal.

Genevieve featured on a stamp for Union Island in St Vincent and the Grenadines, West Indies.

A plastic Airfix model kit of a 1904 Darracq.

Assembled Airfix kit of a 1904 Darracq.

Front-on view of the assembled Airfix kit for a 1904 Darracq.

George and his wife Kathleen arrived in England for the 1957 London to Brighton run, taking part in a 1903 Gladiator owned by the late Mr G James Allday. Later – at a cocktail party, held in the Brighton Pavilion and given by the Lord Mayor of Brighton Alderman C Tyson – they were introduced to Norman Reeves and his wife, who had undertaken the run in a 1899 Benz Dogcart. George was asked to reply to the Veteran Car Club's toast "To our guests for the dinner."

On this particular occasion, Gilltrap had tested the water by suggesting to Norman Reeves that he might consider selling him Genevieve. Not a show, it seemed. Interestingly though, Reeves had already begun to tire of the 'Mr Genevieve' label, and by then had even offered the car to Henry Cornelius and his wife Marjory. They declined, firstly because they didn't have a garage for her, and, secondly, they couldn't find the asking price

of £450; every penny they had owned had been sunk into the movie. A similar offer had also been turned down by the Lord Mayor of Brighton.

In early 1958, Genevieve was sent on loan to Australia for some months, in the care of the late Mr Rex Turner. In March of that year, Mr Turner drove the Darracq in the Blue Mountains Rally, completing it successfully and gaining second place. An estimated 250,000 people saw the event along the 132-mile route from Sydney to Katoomba and back, while 30,000 turned up at Centennial Park for the finish. Only five of the 71 starters failed to return.

This was just about the only rally undertaken in Australia at that time, although the car was used in exhibitions and for advertising purposes. Owing to her success in Australia, Norman Reeves contacted the Gilltraps in New Zealand, enquiring if by any chance they would like to

Continued page 90

From Australian Modern Motor, 1958.

GENEVIEV

This French lady is 53, but she carries her a
a film star, too, and probably the most famous

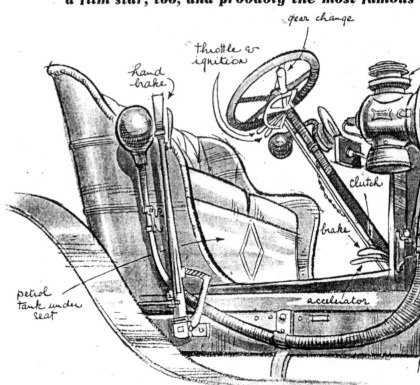

gear change

throttle & ignition

hand brake

clutch

brake

petrol tank under seat

accelerator

Sketches by staff artist Terry Trowell

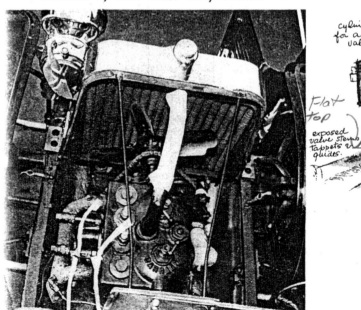

cylinder plug for access to valves

Flat top

exposed valve stems tappets & glides.

is here!

ightly. She's
n the world

"GENEVIEVE," the 1904 Darracq which starred in the highly successful British film of the same name, is at present touring Australia.

Genevieve's English owner, Norman Reeves, has consigned her to the care of Rex Turner, proprietor of Australia's first Veteran Car Museum, in Mosman (Sydney).

The venerable lady's bonnet conceals a sturdy two-cylinder, 12-horsepower engine of 112mm. bore and 120mm. stroke. Unusual touches include priming cocks for cold-weather starting, cylinder plugs for access to the valves (head and block being in one unit), long exposed valve-stems, guides and tappets, and —horror of horrors—a modern Zenith updraught carburettor.

Power is transmitted via a tremendous flywheel and cone clutch, and an equally enormous three-speed

GENEVIEVE as she appeared in the film.

the steering wheel, and a handbrake outside the body.

Dashboard "instrumentation" consists of a total-loss drip-feed oil indicator and metering box, trembler box, and a couple of electrical switches of recent origin.

Genevieve is well provided with horns, having two brass bulb tooters and a natty exhaust siren. She has a huge brass acetylene headlamp, two brass side-lamps cunningly converted to electricity, and two tail-lamps.

Attractively finished in shiny black paint with red lining and red upholstery, Genevieve positively sparkles with bright brass and colorful badges. Her showroom price back in 1904 was £350. Where could you buy a car of such quality at that price to-day? And what 1957 model would you expect to find still running in the year 2010?   • • •

Veteran Car Club of France.

Siren attached to exhaust.

Veteran Car Club of Great Britain.

the 'blind' side!

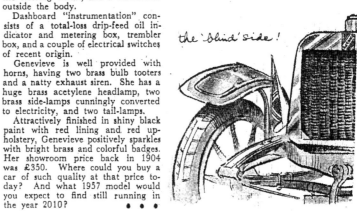

gearbox, to a differential that wouldn't shame a five-ton lorry.

Footbrakes, on rear wheels only, are of the internal expanding type— but the handbrake is contracting and acts on the transmission. Suspension is by half-elliptics. The wood-spoked wheels are shod with 765 by 105mm. beaded-edge tyres.

Gear-changes are made by a sliding-quadrant type lever mounted on the steering column (that's right— nothing new under the sun).

"Office" layout is comparatively conventional, with the normal clutch, brake and accelerator pedals, hand throttle and ignition control levers on

spare tyres on top of tool box.

chassis extension.

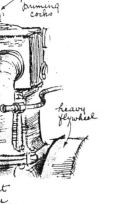

plugs
petrol priming cocks

heavy flywheel

A photo from The Sydney Morning Herald,
March 17th 1958, showing Rex Turner
bringing Genevieve to the
Blue Mountains Rally finishing line.

have Genevieve on loan as Mr Turner had done, particularly as the car was in this part of the world. Failing that, he asked whether they would have any interest in purchasing Genevieve outright. Like a shot, Mr Gilltrap decided on the loan for a start. As a result, Genevieve was shipped from Sydney to Auckland on board the Monowai on May 14th 1958. The crate containing the car was delivered to Rotorua on May 20th, and Mr Gilltrap was able to drive it the same day. With the Darracq came an

Continued page 93

May 20th 1958, George Gilltrap of Rotorua,
New Zealand, drives Genevieve for the first time
upon arrival from Australia.

"CROSSWAYS"

GRAYS PARK ROAD,

STOKE POGES, BUCKS.

FARNHAM COMMON 578.

1st October, 1958

G. E. Gilltrap, Esq.,
Gilltrap's Motor Museum
Gilltrap Street
off Old Taupo Road
Rotorua, NEW ZEALAND

Dear Mr.Gilltrap

I have just returned from my vacation and find your letter of the
19th September with cheque in final settlement for Genevieve.

As requested I am **attaching a brief history** and hope this helps
when you get enquiries.   So far as the license plate is concerned
I can tell you that when I procured the car it had already been licensed
by the finder with an up to date number and despite all my xxxly efforts,
I could not get an early number for the car but after the success of the
film, the licensing authority opened their hearts and produced an early
Middlesex County Council number, which is the one now on the car.
Incidentally, this number should be returned to Gt.Britain as of course
I have the Registration Book here and strictly speaking should notify the
authorities that the number is no longer in circulation in the British
Isles.   Please therefore let me know what you intend to do about
re-registering the car in New Zealand.

Meantime, I send my kind wishes.   If ever I am travelling in your
part of the world, be sure I will call to see you.

Yours sincerely,

Opposite: Letter from Norman Reeves to George Gilltrap, October 1st 1958, regarding final payment for Genevieve and registration plates.

ancient-looking sheet of paper explaining how the vehicle should be started. The original document looks as though it was put together on an equally aged typewriter in need of a new ribbon. Here is a word for word replication:

OPERATING DETAILS

Genevieve

General
Any low detergent 20/40 oil OK
Standard or Super petrol
Tyre pressure Front 40psi Back 40psi

Lubrication by exhaust pressurised dash tank with sight glass. Exhaust to tank pipe requires regular cleaning. Drain tap do not drain sump, just lowers oil level to minimum safe level. Maximum safe level is when exhaust smoke is excessive. Sight glass will need adjusting to suit conditions but I think a drip rate of about 20 per minute is average although I have never counted. Bottom of sight well should be just full and rate will vary with load. By turning tap to horizontal and slowly lifting the pump, the glass tube can be filled with oil. Turn tap to vertical to release oil. This should be done while starting (on full) and to supplement the drip if load is heavy or engine knocks. Excess oil in sump will tend to blow out door in side of block.

Starting
Set spark to retard (top lever towards drivers side)
Set throttle to approximately one quarter.
Bleed carby

Switch on ignition and crank (normally 2 swings only)

A new ignition timer and brush is required (standard 'T' Ford still widely available new) and any poor starting, backfiring etc will be due to timer earthing on retard cable due to wear in the casing. As there is no fan the car will overheat if left running for a period of time while not moving.

Other Points
Engine recently reconditioned and still tight.
Clutch is always very abrupt. Do not try and slip.
Two red cones in boot are universal covers.
Boot lid handle has been temporarily attached, but is normally removed and kept with the driver.
Front wheels need attention before any long trip is attempted.
Original wheels accompany the car.

Throughout New Zealand, Genevieve created great interest indeed, and was the star

George Gilltrap Snr posing with Genevieve.

attraction at auto shows staged by Mr Gilltrap in Rotorua, Masterton, Hamilton, Auckland, and Tauranga during her six months in the country. These auto shows were in aid of charity, and at all times Genevieve accompanied ten other Gilltrap cars and a display of modern vehicles. By this time, George Gilltrap was planning in earnest a move to Australia, in order to set up a museum there. On hearing this, Norman Reeves wrote again, renewing his offer to sell Genevieve. Officially, on October 1st 1958, ownership of the world's best known veteran car passed into the hands of a New Zealander for the reputed price of £1200, somewhat more than the £350 it would have cost when new, 54 years before.

This date has another significance. From his home at Stoke Poges in Buckinghamshire, Mr Reeves wrote to George Gilltrap on that very same day, relating why Genevieve now bore a different registration plate, H399. He explained as follows:

"So far as the licence plate is concerned, I can tell you that when I procured the car it had already been licensed by the finder with an up-to-date number and, despite all my efforts, I could not get an early number for the car, but after the success of the film, the licensing authority opened their hearts and produced an early Middlesex county council number, which is the one now on the car. Incidentally, this number should be returned to Great Britain as of course I have the registration book here, and strictly speaking should notify the authorities that the number is no longer in circulation in the British Isles. Please therefore let me know what you intend to do about re-registering the car in New Zealand."

Once this was attended to, Genevieve bore a simple numerical NZ plate, number 525-894.

The manner in which Genevieve's change of ownership occurred caused a rumpus within the ranks of the UK's veteran car movement. No old car with fame attached to it should be allowed to leave permanently, they argued. The fact that no one knew of a likely sale meant that all those who would have been keen, had they been aware, were automatically precluded. It proved a bitter pill to swallow.

There was one stumbling block to the new deal; the New Zealand government of the day refused to grant a permanent import licence for Genevieve. Only a temporary one could be issued, which in turn helped seal the Gilltrap's decision to move themselves and their car collection to Queensland, Australia.

Once more Genevieve crossed the Tasman, this time from Tauranga to Brisbane. It was July 1959, and a new life in a new country. Her first public showing was the subject of much attention, taking place at a three-day autorama staged in the Brisbane City Hall, as a segment of Queensland's centenary celebrations. The Queensland Bush Childrens' appeal benefited from this to the tune of AUD$2000.

Gilltrap's Auto Museum, on Australia's Gold Coast, was built and eventually opened on September 20th 1959. Visitors were given the opportunity not only to see but also to hear the exhibits in action, which was unheard of then in the majority of similar museums. Even today it is not common. Genevieve, not surprisingly, became quite literally the star attraction. Put on display in front of an artists impression of the English road to Brighton, museum visitors were able to be photographed sitting behind the steering wheel.

Over time, Gilltrap's became one of the country's best known tourist attractions, and George was dubbed the Gold Coast's best ambassador by the Coolangatta Chamber of Commerce. He considered himself fortunate to be able to turn a hobby into a full-time business. Saluting his adopted country, he furthered his interests by establishing an offshoot to car collecting, preserving items of interest from the time he and his family first arrived from New Zealand. So began the museum's extensive Australiana collection.

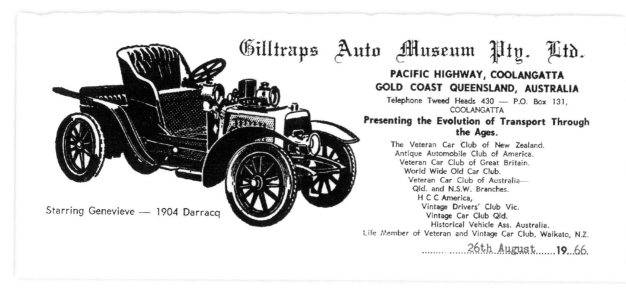

Gilltrap's Auto Museum letterhead.

A carry bag from Gilltrap's museum gift shop.

During her time there, Genevieve carried the Queensland Governor of the day, Sir Henry Abel Smith, and bore the Royal Standard. Larry Adler, on a visit to Brisbane in 1961, rode in her for the first time. She went on to carry many notable figures, while her television appearances both in Australia and New Zealand were numerous.

The early 1960s found George Gilltrap with an incurable health condition. Undaunted, he

Front cover of Gilltrap's Auto Museum handbook – Kirra Beach, Coolangatta, Queensland, Australia – framed by its star attraction.

Genevieve carrying Queensland Governor of the day, Sir Henry Abel Smith, through Surfers Paradise on the Gold Coast, in the early 1960s.

Genevieve being stripped for a rebuild, prior to the 1965 International Rally for Vintage and Veteran Cars, South Island, New Zealand.

pressed on with plans for him and his wife to bring Genevieve back to New Zealand's South Island, in order to partake in the mammoth 1965 International Rally of the International Federation of Veteran Car Clubs, an event that was officially founded on May 29th 1960, in the German city of Wiesbaden. The club's first big event took place twelve months later in the form of the Dutch Jubilee Rally. 1962 saw the German equivalent, and Bognor Regis in England followed during 1963. Italy hosted the 1964 version at Chioggia. The fifth gathering of its type was obviously the first to be held outside Europe, and a huge leap not only in distance but in organisational planning. This had begun in December 1963 for a 1300-mile tour, billed as being 'a competitive tour of the Haast Pass, southern lakes and goldfields of New Zealand.' In other words, a journey through some of the most spectacular scenery anywhere on earth.

To prepare for such a gruelling event, George stripped the Darracq down for a total rebuild. In doing so it was discovered that only two worn clutch pins could have prevented Genevieve from partaking in the rally. It was at this point that the collection of dashboard medals, which had previously adorned the facia, were unaccountably removed and placed

Continued page 103

The Darracq in pieces.

The Gilltraps pause on the drive between Coolangatta and Sydney en route to New Zealand.

George and Kathleen Gilltrap leave their Queensland museum, bound for New Zealand and the 1965 South Island rally.

*George Gilltrap Snr at the starting line of the 1965 International Rally for
Vintage and Veteran Cars, Christchurch, New Zealand.*

on a freestanding board beside the car in the museum. They joined other similar displays depicting the Darracq's heyday as a film star and weren't, regrettably, returned to the dash for another 28 years. Not content with the rally driving that lay ahead, the Gilltraps – with a good deal of local fanfare – set off from Coolangatta, bound for New Zealand by way of a 600-mile drive south from the Gold Coast to Sydney. From there they sailed for Auckland, driving Genevieve down through the North Island to Wellington. En route, an incident at Turangi all but put paid to

Opposite: Front cover of the catalogue for the 1965 International Rally for Vintage and Veteran Cars, in the South Island of New Zealand.

the reason for their journey, when a cleaning rag left by mistake on the engine caught fire. Flames leapt two feet into the air, and not until a certain amount of roadside clay had been thrown over it was the fire eventually extinguished.

Without further incident Genevieve and her passengers crossed from the North to the South Island, and were lined up at the rally starting post in Christchurch's Addington Show Grounds on March 6th. The selfsame spot welcomed their return on March 18th, having successfully completed the adventure of a lifetime that took place in-between. New Zealand entrants were joined by those from Australia, South Africa, America, Holland, Malaysia, and Great Britain;

Continued page 106

*George and Genevieve at Lake Pukaki,
in the rugged high country of
New Zealand's South Island.*

The Gilltraps head through the Haast section of the 1965 International South Island rally.

these entrants included Lord Montagu of Beaulieu, in his 1913 Prince Henry Vauxhall, and Miss Elizabeth Nagle, an eminent British authority and author on vintage motoring. Before leaving the lovely garden city of Christchurch, one press commentator referred to the gathering as "blood and thunder amongst the veterans."

Competing vehicles ventured by way of such famous beauty spots as Mount Cook, Lake Wanaka, the Haast Pass, Arrowtown, Queenstown, Te Anau, Milford Sound, and Dunedin. Of the 294 cars that set out, 288 made it back to Christchurch under their own steam. This was as much a tribute to the ruggedness of the four-wheeled contestants as it was to those who had prepared and maintained them. The cars competed for several awards; the premier accolade was The Haans Georg School Memorial Trophy of the International Federation of Veteran Car Clubs. Len Southward of Wellington, driving a 1912 Buick, scooped this award for losing the least amount of points in the whole event. Len had previously won the same award in Germany in 1962 for having the best-prepared car. The North Island motor museum that bore his name was well known in New Zealand; in it, he displayed a Darracq the same vintage as Genevieve.

CHAPTER
THIRTEEN

The rally was divided into nine classes. Gold plaque awards were presented to all class winners, and to each of the five section winners. Those in second place received silver plaques, whilst the bronze equivalent went to all who completed the course. Each plaque showed an old Darracq service car, set against a background of the Southern Alps. Darracqs, interestingly enough, had been used extensively in New Zealand's early days of pioneer motoring, especially in the uncharted high country where anything or anyone had to be of a robust nature to ensure survival.

Genevieve's participation was a huge rally drawcard. She attracted tremendous interest, particularly as the film was reissued to coincide with the event.

Despite her star status Genevieve, through sheer robustness, found herself second overall in the Veteran section when the rally eventually wound up, two weeks after it had started. Interviewed in Christchurch at that time, George said he would never part with his film star car. He reasoned that to do so would be like losing a member of his family. Sadly 12 months later, in 1966, George Gilltrap lost his own life after suffering from leukaemia. His wishlist had included completing the previous year's New Zealand rally. He also wanted to drive Genevieve back to Queensland along the same route that he and Kathleen had travelled on their outward journey. Both were achieved. Fortunately, there had been time to prepare for the fate that lay in store for this family. George Gilltrap Jnr stepped in to carry on what his father had begun, thus ensuring the survival of Gilltrap's Auto Museum, a business that had been developed with plenty of entrepreneurial expertise and showmanship.

During the next 20 years, those visiting the museum at Kirra Beach, Coolangatta, could – for a small fee – continue to clamber up and be photographed behind the wheel of the 'movie star car.'

In 1981, it was deemed appropriate to move the entire museum to the new Gold Coast Disney-style theme park known as Dreamworld. Here, a special Genevieve display was set up. Scenes from the film sat alongside the car, including the 31 dashboard badges depicting rallies in Belgium, France, England, Germany, Sweden, and Luxembourg, in which she had participated during the Norman Reeves years.

Following the unexpected passing of Mrs Kathleen Gilltrap in 1989, it was decided to put the Gilltrap auto collection up for auction. This wasn't exactly a joint family decision. Two brothers and

Continued page 112

Driving between Lake Wanaka and Cromwell on the central South Island leg of the international rally.

*A 'rare' view, as Genevieve hits the road between Te Anau and Milford Sound
on her journey around New Zealand's South Island.*

1913 Morris Takes Lead From Genevieve in Rally

16/3/65

P.A.

INVERCARGILL, To-day.

A SMALL veteran car from Hawke's Bay, N. E. Findlay's 1913 Morris, has lost the least points and is leading for the Schoof Memorial Trophy, the major prize in the sixth international vintage car rally.

The small Morris had gone ahead of the film star car, Genevieve, the 1904 Darracq driven by G Giltrap, of Queensland, in the light veteran class by putting up a better time on the run from Wanaka to the Pleasant Flat bridge on the Haast Road.

Most of the results calculated to date are based on driving performance, but some of the tests on the way are included.

Leading positions to date are:

Veteran cars (up to December 1918) having one, two or three cylinders, or having four or more cylinders under 1500 c.c.—N. E. Findlay's 1913 Morris Oxford (Hawke's Bay) 336; G. Giltrap's Auto Museum's 1904 Darracq (Genevieve) Queensland, 423; J. A. McLachlan's 1907 Cadillac (Southbridge) 798.

Veteran cars, 1500 c.c. and under 300 c.c.—J. G. Watson's 1909 Clement Talbot (Wellington) 370; C. R. Hervey's 1918 Chevrolet (South Canterbury) 478; G. B. Gelf's 1915 Ford (Canterbury) 483.

Veteran cars, 300 c.c. and over.—R. Oakley's 1912 Regzl (Otago) 484; J. Newell's 1911 Wolseley (Canterbury) 487; Montagu of Beaulieu's 1914 Prince Henry Vauxhall (Britain) 520.

Vintage cars (1919 to December, 1930) under 1500 c.c.—E. Galt's 1926 Fiat (Canterbury) 448; L. Nye's 1930 Austin (Otago) 515; P. Shaskey's 1925 O. M. (Canterbury) 529.

Vintage cars 1500 c.c. and under 2000 c.c.—K. M. Newberry's 1923 Ansaldo (Canterbury) 525, A. A. Dray's 1928 Alvis (Wellington) 558; D. W. Jordan's 1923 Sunbeam (Southland) 616.

Vintage cars 2000 c.c. and under 3000 c.c.—P. K. Andrews 1928 Chevrolet (Manawatu) 4 K. C. McMillan's 1929 Vauxhall (Southland) 472; M. H. Haggitt's 1925 Bentley (Otago) 476; W. Clapham's 1920 Stanley Steamer (Canterbury) 478.

Vintage cars, 3000 c.c. and under 4000 c.c.—D. D. Hilland's 1929 Chevrolet (Otago) 460; B. R. Lay's 1922 Rolls Royce (Hawke's Bay) 505; E. K. Newman's 1928 Dodge (Canterbury) 531; J. Williamson's 1930 For (Canterbury) 540.

Vintage cars 4000 c.c. and over. — R. A. Kilbey's 193 Chrysler (Hawke's Bay) 540 A. B. Seccombe's 1930 Bentley (Auckland) 578; J. W. Rowley' 1926 Vauxhall (Britain) 588 H. R. Hagan's 1924 Vauxhall (N.S.W.) 631.

Vintage and veteran motorcycles.—R. Belk's 1929 A.J.S. (Manawatu) 410 points lost; I. T. Barnes's 1910 Triumph (South Canterbury) 520; A. G. Taylor's 1916 Triumph (Canterbury) 662.

Wounded

Two members of the newly-arrived United States Marine Brigade guarding the American Air Base in Da Nang (South Vietnam) were seriously wounded last night. They were believed to be in a clash with Viet Cong guerrillas.—N.Z.-P.A.-Reuter.

Genevieve loses her rally lead as this newspaper account explains.

George Gilltrap lines up his 1904 Darracq alongside E R Robins, from Cave near Timaru, in his 1906 car of the same make.

Kathleen Gilltrap docking in upon returning to Christchurch after completing the March 1965 New Zealand International Rally.

An advert from New Zealand's Christchurch Star newspaper, promoting a display of all competing vehicles at the rally's conclusion.

one sister were the proponents behind the move. A remaining sibling felt that their father's dream was being forfeited when, after his death, they had all worked so hard to preserve it. Nevertheless, news of the forthcoming auction, described as 'Australia's foremost collection,' drew national and international attention. One family member felt all this may have been a bit hasty, given that there were to be no reserve prices and, after further in-house discussions, the sale may not have gone ahead; in the end, the sale went forward.

A total of 550 lots fetched AUD$2.5 million. A huge cheer went up when it was realised that Genevieve would after all be staying in Australia, having been purchased for a record AUD$580,000 by entrepreneur Paul Terry. Terry had originally founded a financial services company in Sydney,

later selling that business to retire in Albany, a one-time whaling port south of Perth in Western Australia. Another nine possible buyers had been bidding, mostly by phone, from overseas; these people dropped by the wayside, however, when the price reached AUD$350,000. This included Lord Montagu of the UK's National Motor Museum, at Beaulieu in Hampshire. Not unnaturally, he had always hoped that the day might come when the world's most celebrated veteran car would find a home in his equally famed motoring collection, originally set up in 1952 when the film Genevieve went into production. A representative of Lord

Continued page 115

Opposite: A promotional shot in the Kirra Beach sand hills, Coolangatta, Queensland.

At Gilltrap's Queensland Auto Museum 1974. Genevieve as displayed, with all badges – once on the dash – now consigned to a display board to the bottom left. The author at the wheel, with Colin Whyte from New Zealand.

The author driving Genevieve in 1977, Coolangatta, Queensland.

George Gilltrap Jnr and the author's wife in Genevieve at 'Dream World,' on Queensland's Gold Coast, after Gilltrap's museum moved there from Coolangatta in 1981.

Montagu, while visiting Australia in 1984, had approached the Gilltraps about the prospects of buying the Darracq.

Five years later, and with the car due to be auctioned, all stops were pulled out to raise whatever funds might be needed to secure a purchase, and a tentative earlier bid was unsuccessful. Ultimately, the National Motor Museum simply didn't have the money ready to put enough of a financial stake in the ground for Genevieve. In turn, they approached a half-dozen or so companies who could possibly, for various reasons, benefit from buying the car. For just as many reasons, it seems they all declined. After all, with no reserve, how high would one have to go? The National Motor Museum Trust newsletter of October 1989 reported that a local enthusiast asked the museum if it could house and show Genevieve, were he to be the new owner. "Oh yes indeed," came the reply. Sadly, the enthusiast also had no luck, and it wasn't all to do with lack of funds. He was due to bid by phone, and had arranged for the auctioneer to put a call through at the appropriate time during the selling process.

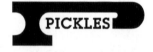

The World Famous

GILLTRAP MUSEUM
COLLECTION

to be sold at Unreserved Auction

Under Instruction From
George Gilltrap, Robyn Hadley and Kevin Gilltrap
as Directors of Gilltraps Auto Museum Pty. Ltd. following the death of
Mrs. Kathleen Gilltrap.

10.00am SUNDAY AUGUST 20th 1989

at

The Magic Millions Gold Coast Sales and

Convention Centre

Ascot Court

Gold Coast

Queensland Australia

Refer Map page 31

Inspection:

Saturday & Sunday 12th & 13th August

Friday & Saturday 18th & 19th August

10.00 a.m. to 4.00 p.m.

About 20 other suitable exotic vehicles will be sold on
behalf of other Vendors. An Addendum will be issued
closer to sale and will be posted on request.

Admission to Auction by catalogue only.

1

George Gilltrap Jnr takes a last nostalgic look at Genevieve prior to the '89 auction.

As (bad) luck would have it, a telephone problem on the Gold Coast stopped calls going in several directions, including to Beaulieu. From this, it could be assumed that being there on the spot in person, if you are really keen, is not a bad idea.

With everyone else out of the running, it came down to Paul Terry and fellow Australian Robert Holmes a'Court, also on a long distant line.

Opposite: Announcing the auction of Gilltrap's Auto Museum collection, August 1989.

Mr a'Court remained philosophical in losing out. "When it was over, there was no blood left in my hand, because I was gripping the phone so hard and shaking all over. Bugatti Royales fetch up to $16 million, and there were six of them built. Genevieve is the most famous car in the world and is unique." Terry's winning bid was at the time a world record for a two-cylinder veteran car. It was just one of several world record prices at the Gilltrap auction.

Paul Terry did not personally attend the Gilltrap auction, although he had previously been

New owner Paul Terry, in Genevieve, is pushed into an Albany, West Australia, media appearance following the Darracq's arrival from the Queensland auction.

to look the vehicles over. When doing so, he had told George Gilltrap Jnr that he wasn't particularly interested in buying Genevieve. George had been quite matter of fact in explaining that maintenance on the car had slipped somewhat, and there was plenty that needed doing. It was Paul's wife Joan who urged him to change his mind and to bid at all costs. Having arranged the delivery of their new purchase to Western Australia, Genevieve let them down by not firing up on command. Manpower had to be employed to move her into position for her appearance in Albany, the first in front of the public and the media.

FOURTEEN

The Terrys possessed tremendous flair. Together they shared a mutual love of art and collectables. They had built the beautiful colonial-style Esplanade Hotel and Extravaganza Gallery at Albany, designed to display fabulous paintings and ceramics, fine furniture, wine and – of course – automobiles, including Marilyn Monroe's Cadillac and a twin pair of Hooper-bodied Rolls-Royces used for royal and civic occasions. Cars, argued Paul, were indisputably one of the greatest forms of three-dimensional sculpture. Sculpture that moves, sounds and smells.

When Genevieve arrived from Queensland, and he took a closer look at his latest acquisition, Paul was horrified. She really did need attention.

The engine had all but given up the ghost. There was so much play in the drive line that, when the clutch was engaged, the driver would have to wait for everything to be taken up before moving forward. Both crankcase and block were cracked, requiring delicate metal stitching in places that had already been repaired several times.

While the engine was undoubtedly in poor shape, even disregarding the fragile state of its

Continued page 122

Left & overleaf: Genevieve being rebuilt under the Terrys' ownership.

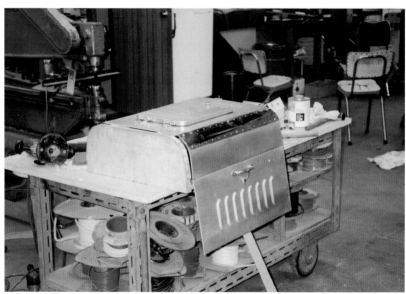

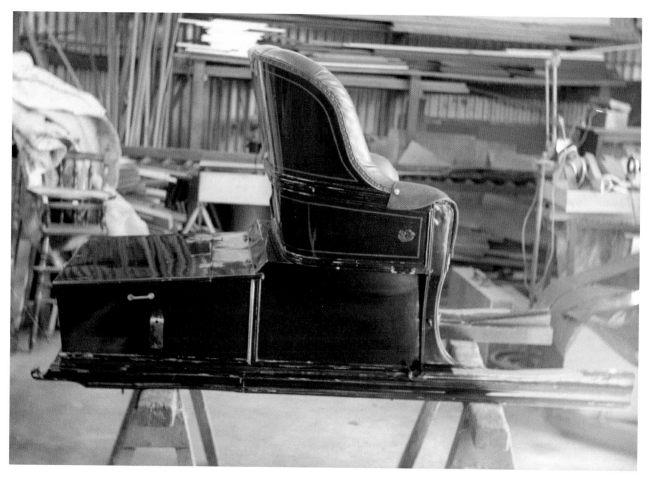

original crankcase, it was nevertheless rebuilt. As it happens, a spare 1905 pattern engine with a more robust iron crankcase is available to be fitted for non-Brighton runs, breathing – one hopes – a longer lifespan into the original.

The differential was likewise a nightmare for Paul Terry's restorer, Ken Taylor, who put it like this:

"[It was] primitive to say the least, owing to there being no adjustment for preload, as everything is fitted in with the shims. The only way to tell if it's right is to fully assemble it, and if there's a problem the whole lot has to come apart again. It's all ball bearings too, so as you assemble it, you have to grease the cups, put all the balls in position and fit it together, just like a bicycle. The cone clutch was re-leathered and the main gear wheels on the axle and gearbox cogs had to be remade. It's very hard to put the right pitch on such gears – modern machinery just can't handle it.

"The majority of the body timber is original, but the crude seats (previously sheeted up in alloy) were remade, and the upholstery was redone in leather. The non-original 12-spoke wheels, always something of a talking point, were retained and rebuilt. George Gilltrap Jnr is fairly certain that Genevieve's front wheels, at least, were from a Model T Ford when Paul Terry took ownership. But George believed they were fitted in the mid-1970s, after the wheels that were on the car were damaged when his brother was in Melbourne with Genevieve for promotional reasons. The damaged wheels were retained, and went with the Darracq to Western Australia in 1989. Whether these were the original ones on the car when it arrived in New Zealand from England in the late 1950s is not a hundred per cent certain. Perhaps Henry Ford has more to answer for than he realises!"

Basically, Terry's instruction to Ken Taylor had been to give Genevieve a total restoration while at the same time preserving her movie image, and to have her maintained exactly as she had always been known to her millions of admirers worldwide. Paul Terry was firmly of the opinion that Genevieve's fame lay in her film star status, and not as a genuine period Darracq. This included a decision not to use a 1904 chassis and gearbox purchased with the car from the Gilltraps. Doing so would have contributed to bringing the Darracq closer to its original production specifications, but for Paul "It was a snappy move I didn't allow myself too long to think about, she was more important as a film star car than anything else."

At the time of this rebuild, Genevieve was carefully examined by a committee of experts from the Veteran Car Club of Australia. They confirmed the date of 1904, which she had been given by the Veteran Car Club of Great Britain while she was in Norman Reeves' ownership. She had been listed under that date in every subsequent Veteran Car Club register of Veteran and Edwardian Cars. To support this evidence, she has the dating certificate of the VCCA, which works to the same meticulous standards and is recognised as a competent authority by the Veteran Car Club of Great Britain.

Meanwhile, Paul Terry was in the process of establishing the Genevieve 500, the first truly international race for veteran and vintage cars; an occasion intended to rival the 1987 America's Cup held off the coast of Fremantle near Perth. If all went well, the Genevieve 500 would become an annual event. The inaugural race was earmarked to take place in November 1992, and would feature 100 cars and their drivers from around the world. Mr Terry himself offered to subsidise freight costs for the first three cars entered from each country. Rich prizes would be competed for, in what was

Continued page 125

2.00 fee required

THE VETERAN CAR CLUB OF W.A.

VEHICLE REGISTRATION AND DATING FORM

Please complete this form in BLOCK CAPITALS and return it, together with at least ONE good photograph of the car, to the Secretary

I wish to apply for the date of the following car to be certified by the Committee and enclose................photograph(s.)

Note: Unless at least one good photograph is sent, the dating may be considerably delayed. (Those taken before restoration are of much greater use.)

PAUL TERRY INTERNATIONAL PTY LIMITED

Name and Address of Member.........PO Box 1407. ALBANY. WA. 6330......... A.C.N. 801 185 300

(P.G. WARTON *RAMAN DIRECTOR — MEMBER OF VCC of WA*)

GENERAL PARTICULARS OF CAR

1. Make. DARRACQ .... 2. Registration Number ....
3. Claimed Year of Manufacture,..... 1904 .... 4. Maker's H.P. 12
5. Car No. (if any) and where inscribed. BRASS PLATE ON DASH BOARD ENGLISH Nº 743
   CHASSIS Nº 6505

PARTICULARS OF ENGINE

A. GENERAL:

1. Engine No. and where inscribed... 6060 ..... TOP OF CRANKCASE AT FRONT
2. Cylinder Bore........ 112 MM .... 3. Piston stroke... 120 MM
   No. of Cylinders.. TWO .... 5. If a Multi-cylinder engine, whether monobloc, cast
6. Are Cylinder Heads detachable.. NO .... in threes, pairs, or singly... MONOBLOC
7. Position of Engine. .. .. FRONT .... 8. Vertical or Horizontal... VERTICAL

B. COOLING:

9. Is Engine Air-cooled or Water-cooled...... WATER COOLED
10. If the latter, is a Pump fitted and how is is Driven. INTERNAL CHAIN DRIVEN PUMP.
11. Is there a Fan ...... NO
12. Position of Radiator and/or Water Tank. RADIATOR MOUNTED IN FRONT OF ENGINE
13. Type of Radiator, Honeycomb or Gilled Tube. GILLED TUBE

C. VALVES:

14. Are inlet valves automatic (suction operated) or mechanical.. MECHANICAL
15. If mechanical, are there 1 or 2 camshafts. If 1, is it N/S or O/S. 1 CAMSHAFT N/S
16. If mechanical, are they Side or O.H ...... SIDE
17. Is engine fitted with a Governor or are there signs of one having been fitted. WAS ORIGINALLY FITTED WITH GOVERNOR BUT NOW MISSING.

D. CARBURETTION:

18. Type and Make of Carburettor. CLAUDEL HOBSON
19. Is fuel supply by pressure or gravity.. GRAVITY
20. If pressure, Air or Exhaust. ....

E. IGNITION:

21. Type of Ignition System: (Tube, Trembler coil, L.T. Mag. or H.T. Mag.). TREMBLER COILS

F. LUBRICATION:

22. Type of Lubrication to Engine. (Splash, Hand-pump, Drip Feed or Mechanical system). SPLASH. HAND PUMP AND DRIP FEED.

PARTICULARS OF TRANSMISSION

A. CLUTCH:

1. Is it Cone, Plate or other type.... CONE

B. GEAR BOX (if fitted)

2. Type of Gear Box. (Sliding, Epicyclic, Expanding clutch, Friction disc or Belts and Pulleys). SLIDING NUMBER 368
3. Position of Gear Lever. STEERING COLUMN 4. Gate or Quadrant type. R.N. 1 2 3 IN LINE
5. No. of forward speeds. THREE 6. Is there a reverse. YES
7. If so, is it controlled by a separate lever. ONLY ONE LEVER

C. FINAL DRIVE:

8. System used. (Shaft, Central chain, 2 side chains, Belt or a combination of these). SHAFT
9. If Shaft, Open Shaft or Torque Tube.. OPEN SHAFT
10. If Shaft, is it Bevel or Worm drive. BEVEL DRIVE

Above & overleaf: The VCC of Western Australia's vehicle registration and official dating form for Genevieve, following Paul Terry's full restoration.

PARTICULARS OF CHASSIS

A. GENERAL:

1. Chassis No. and where inscribed : . . . .
2. Is frame Tubular, Channel Steel or Wood and Flitch-plate type. *PRESSED STEEL*
3. Track . *FRONT* 4 ft. 4½ ins.   4. Wheelbase . . . . 7 ft. 4½ ins.
   REAR 4 FT ½ INS

B. SUSPENSION:

5. Is it by ¼, ½, ¾ or Full-elliptic, Cantilever, Coil or Transverse springing
   Front . *HALF ELLIPTIC* . . . . Rear . *HALF ELLIPTIC*

C. STEERING:

6. Wheel or Tiller . *WHEEL* . . . .   7. Position of column *OFF SIDE*
   (N/S, O/S or Central)
8. Vertical or Inclined. *INCLINED* . . . . .   9. Is Track-rod in front of *BEHIND*
   or behind front axle . . .
10. Is Front Axle H-Section, Round or Square . *ROUND*

D. BRAKES:

11. State whether on Transmission, Drums or Tyres and type (Contracting, Expanding or Spoon)
    Foot Brake. *DRUM ON REAR OF TRANS*   Hand Brake. *REAR WHEEL DRUMS EXPANDING*
    EXPANDING
12. Does Hand Brake pull or push on. . . . . . . *PUSH ON*

E. WHEELS AND TYRES:

13. Wood, Wire or Steel Artillery type. *WOOD*
14. Whether quickly detachable. *NO*
15. No. of Spokes (Wood or Artillery only) Front. *12* . . . Rear . *12*
16. Size of Tyres. Front. *30* x *3½* . Rear. *820* x *120*
17. Solid or Pneumatic. If solid, state diam. of wheels. Front. *PNEUMATIC* . Rear. *PNEUMATIC*

F. COACHWORK

18. Type of Body. . . . .   19. Coachbuilder. . . . .
20. No. of Seats. *TWO* . . . . . .   21. Colour. *CHASSIS RED, BODY + GUARDS BLACK*
22. Are Mudguards Wood, Metal or Leather-covered Metal . *METAL*
23. Mention any Fitting. (Hood, Windscreen, Spare Wheel or Stepney). . . . .
. . . .

G. LIGHTING, Etc.:

24. Type of Lighting System. *DETAILS BELOW*   25. Is a Starter fitted. *NO*

Please give below, full details of all inscriptions on plates, hub-caps, badges, etc., which may exist on the car, particulars of any known modifications and any evidence in support of the claimed year of manufacture, also average running speed of vehicle.

ONE SELF GENERATING GAS HEAD LIGHT. (LUCAS DUPLEX)

TWO KERO SIDE LIGHTS (LUCAS N° 764)

ONE KERO TAIL LIGHT (GEORGE W HOUK LTD)

IT APPEARS CHASSIS HAS BEEN MODIFIED SLIGHTLY TO PERMIT FULL MOVEMENT OF STEERING PITMAN ARM.

Date. . . . .   Signed. . . . .

Genevieve and Marilyn Monroe's Cadillac top extravaganza list

Buyers have so far snapped up four of the 60 classic cars which, together with works of applied and decorative art in the Esplanade Extravaganza gallery, are all for sale including Paul Terry's most valuable possession, Genevieve.

But with a value of AUD25 million he doesn't think the 1904 Darracq, which he calls "the most important car in the world" will change hands in a rush.

It makes Marilyn Monroe's 1962 white Fleetwood Cadillac with a price tag of AUD110,000, seem a bargain.

Marilyn's Cadillac and Genevieve, the star of the 1953 film of the same name, are among 60 vintage cars and more than 600 exhibits on display on two levels of the Esplanade Extravaganza, which also incorporates a large function centre capable of catering for up to 400 people

Admission to the gallery is AUD7 for adults and AUD12 for a family of two adults and two children. Every-

Paul Terry's prized possession – Genevieve – he values at AUD25m.

one visiting Extravaganza will be given a free book called `Classics for Collectors' which details the gallery showcase.

*A new international motoring event – the `Genevieve 500' race - for

vintage and veteran cars will take place in November 1992.

More than 60 pre-1930 cars, including Genevieve, will compete in the genuine handicap speed race between Perth and Albany.

An article noting that Paul Terry valued Genevieve at $25m AUD in 1991.

intended to be a true handicap speed race and not merely just another glorified rally. The handicap system would ensure that each car competed on equal terms to win an overall prize, which took the form of a solid gold replica of Genevieve worth thousands of dollars. Those in second and third place would be handed silver and bronze replicas respectively.

The route – from Perth's Hyatt Regency Hotel, heading 500 kilometres to Albany's beautiful Esplanade Hotel and Extravaganza Gallery on Australia's most southern tip – would take the participants through spectacular countryside. Planned stopovers included the historic town of York for New Orleans jazz and Creole cuisine, Narrogin for a traditional Aussie party (with

damper, kangaroo steaks, and washed down with billy tea), and Katanning for the Genevieve 500 country talent quest. The plan was to race the cars in four one-day stages, recapturing the spirit and style of yesteryear; a grand event in the tradition of the London to Brighton run, and the Great American Race. The whole idea of it all was geared as a tribute to Genevieve herself and organised under the charter of the Confederation of Australian Motorsport, who deemed that no cash prizes should be offered for fear that this might act as an incentive to modify vehicles likely to be entered. All entrants would compete for the country they represented and for the glory of winning the Genevieve Nations Cup, a perpetual trophy going to the country whose three leading contestants achieved the highest combined finishing position. As a further nostalgic tribute to earlier times, a vintage steam train was lined up ready to start and keep pace with all four-wheeled competitors throughout the race. Attached to the engine were sleeping carriages that entrant drivers could use as overnight accommodation after a testing day behind the wheel.

The race was destined to end by the sea at Albany's five-star Esplanade Hotel, followed by a night of revelry and celebration. This was billed as Australia's biggest ever beach party, with entertainment by world-class performers and followed by a gala presentation of awards. Profits from the race were to go to the Genevieve Foundation, the name given to a charitable organisation founded in 1987 by Paul Terry to help those who have no one or nowhere to turn to when they need it most. He guaranteed that a minimum of AUD$100,000 would be donated to the foundation from the first Genevieve 500 of November 1992.

CHAPTER
FIFTEEN

Organisers of the race received a letter of recognition from the Australian Prime Minister of the day, John Keating. He explained that he was delighted to have the opportunity of supporting the inaugural Genevieve 500 International Classic Car Race. Mr Keating also noted that the inception of the race exemplified the spirit of Australian endeavour.

Many significant cars lined up to participate in the first event. These included the 1904 Dutch-built Spyker, brought from Holland to be paired up with Genevieve for the first time since the making of the film in 1952. Gone, though, was its famous daffodil yellow body, long since replaced by an all-new livery in emerald green. There is a point of interest here in relation to the Spyker's colour scheme; some years ago Bill Peacock sent the author a photograph showing a 1898 Daimler, together with the beautifully restored Spyker and his superb Argyll, originally rescued from the Leyton dump. All three were lined up one behind the other ready to start on their way to a 1947 rally in London's Regent Park, but the Spyker appears to be the shade of green it is now.

Enter one Elaine Lemon, daughter of Frank Reece. Reece was the one who made the Spyker available for filming in 1952, appeared in crowd scenes in Hyde Park along with his wife, and

gingerly guided Kenneth More into understanding how to drive the back-firing Dutch veteran. Elaine explained that her father was very proud of the car, which he had originally purchased for £20, spent years restoring and chose to paint the shade of green we see today. Having offered it as Genevieve's on-screen competitor, he became somewhat sceptical over the idea of a rather large, droopy-eyed dog occupying the back seat, and what might its claws do to the leather upholstery. As if this wasn't enough to ponder on, Frank was surprised to find that producer Henry Cornelius believed the early 1950s Technicolor process couldn't do justice to the Spyker's colour scheme; yellow would be better. Reece, having got his head around the canine passenger, reluctantly also agreed to this reasoning, providing that his pride and joy was repainted the original colour once filming was over. His happiness with the way it all turned out prompted Elaine's father to donate the fee he received, for the use of his car in the movie, to the VCC.

The great weekend of November 18th to 21st 1992 arrived with some of the coldest, most unseasonable weather in living memory. Media coverage of the first ever Genevieve 500 was considerable; the sole surviving member of the cast from the celebrated movie, Dinah Sheridan –

Continued page 130

Cover of presentation material promoting Paul Terry's Genevieve 500 race for veteran and vintage cars, running from Perth to Albany, Western Australia, November 1992.

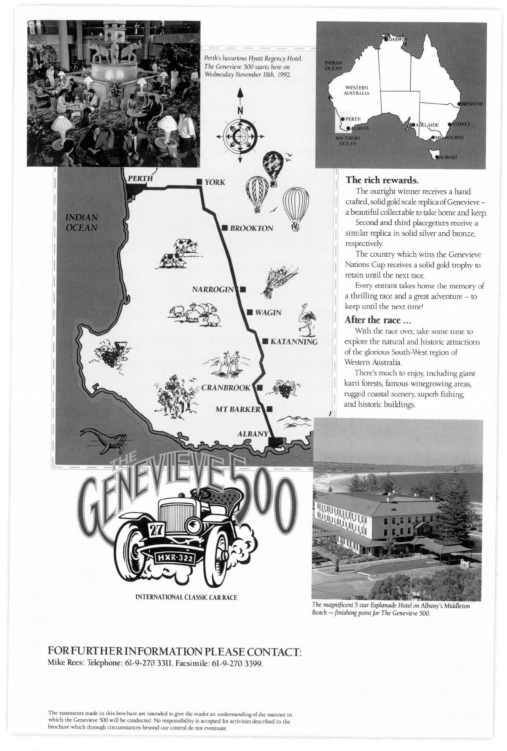

Perth's luxurious Hyatt Regency Hotel. The Genevieve 500 starts here on Wednesday November 18th, 1992.

PERTH ■ YORK

INDIAN OCEAN

■ BROOKTON

NARROGIN ■

■ WAGIN

■ KATANNING

CRANBROOK ■

MT BARKER ■

ALBANY

THE GENEVIEVE 500
INTERNATIONAL CLASSIC CAR RACE

The rich rewards.

The outright winner receives a hand crafted, solid gold scale replica of Genevieve – a beautiful collectable to take home and keep.

Second and third placegetters receive a similar replica in solid silver and bronze, respectively.

The country which wins the Genevieve Nations Cup receives a solid gold trophy to retain until the next race.

Every entrant takes home the memory of a thrilling race and a great adventure – to keep until the next time!

After the race ...

With the race over, take some time to explore the natural and historic attractions of the glorious South-West region of Western Australia.

There's much to enjoy, including giant karri forests, famous winegrowing areas, rugged coastal scenery, superb fishing, and historic buildings.

The magnificent 5 star Esplanade Hotel on Albany's Middleton Beach — finishing point for The Genevieve 500.

FOR FURTHER INFORMATION PLEASE CONTACT:
Mike Rees: Telephone: 61-9-270 3311. Facsimile: 61-9-270 3399.

The road south for the '92 Genevieve 500, en route to Albany from Perth.

Taking part in the 1992 West Australian Genevieve 500, closely followed by the Spyker.

still a head turner at 72 – had reluctantly declined to attend, as the weekend in question clashed with her own special celebration, her wedding and subsequent honeymoon cruise. Instead, the popular local television presenter Susan Carr took the run as Genevieve's passenger. Like Dinah in the film she froze to the bone, reporting that one didn't exactly ride *in* the ancient Darracq, it was more a case of riding *on* her!

Dinah was kept fully informed of the inaugural Genevieve 500's resounding success, and agreed to participate a year later in November 1993. Sadly, it wasn't to be; the first race turned out to also be the last. During that following year Paul Terry was planning to downsize some of his auto collection by selling off his post-World War One vehicles, so that he might concentrate on veteran cars that

would compliment Genevieve. One of his other passions concerned a private airport, wherein he housed a dream variety of fast aircraft. Tragically, at the beginning of July 1993, he died in a freak accident when his helicopter crashed during his first solo flight over Hawaii. The contents of Paul's estate were eventually put up for auction, whilst it had been decided that Genevieve – for the first time since leaving in 1958 – should be sent back to England, and put under the hammer there.

Her homecoming was perfectly timed to coincide with that year's London to Brighton

Opposite: October 1993. Genevieve is back in England for the first time since 1958, and on show at The National Motor Museum, Beaulieu, Hampshire.

rally. The organisers made great capital of this from the publicity viewpoint, and succeeded in drawing huge public attention to the event. Not bad, when one considers that a past president and chairman of the VCC is on record as referring to this particular make of vehicle as being "a miserable little car and a gutless wonder." He later qualified his remarks by agreeing that its fame lay in its film star status, not as a miserable little Darracq.

Before the event could happen, though, Genevieve was taken down to Hampshire, where – by arrangement with Lord Montagu – she was put on display at the National Motor Museum at Beaulieu, in the heart of the New Forest. Such a timely promotional move, in the 40th year of the film's release, didn't exactly go unnoticed.

To capitalise on the significance of Genevieve's return to England, Lord Montagu hosted a dinner party at his home, Palace House, on the Beaulieu Estate. His guests, who later in the evening became guest speakers, included Marjory Cornelius and this author as Genevieve's historian. We were graciously put up at his Lordship's expense in the beautiful Montagu Arms Hotel, in the nearby village. Also included in the guest speaker line-up was Larry Adler, who almost 20 years earlier had contacted Mr and Mrs Gilltrap to discuss his own plans for a new television series, with Genevieve as its leading player. Larry had apparently been in discussions with the original film's copyright owners, Rank Films, on such a possibility. The Gilltraps were happy to make their star car available, providing she wouldn't be away for too long. After all, Genevieve was their museum's main attraction. Nothing more was heard from Mr Adler, so it seems, or plans for his TV venture.

CHAPTER
SIXTEEN

Following a most enjoyable meal at Lord Montagu's table, we all crossed to the Museum Lecture Theatre. Once there, before 200 Friends of the National Motor Museum, Mrs Tania Rose (widow of screenplay writer William Rose), Elizabeth Nagle, other motoring notables, and Genevieve herself, a panel discussion took place that, in effect, charted the Darracq's known history as a car. The not-so-small fact that she became a film star in a movie that ultimately became an unexpected piece of entertainment folklore was obviously not overlooked either.

A few days later, in London, I was present at the Clapham Common West Side establishment of Brooks, the auctioneer. There I watched the late Paul Terry's restoration expert Ken Taylor direct Genevieve's arrival by carrier from the National Motor Museum. Ken was anxious to put the car through her paces, and invited me to climb up beside him before we chugged off in search of a petrol station. It had been some years back, in Australia, that I had last been passenger or driver of Genevieve, so this was a special treat. It was clearly the same for those whom we passed and who pointed incredulously saying to each other, "There's Genevieve."

On Saturday November 7th, with Ken Taylor again at the wheel, Genevieve lined up in Hyde Park for the start of the 1993 London to Brighton Veteran Car Run followed by a faultless rerun, the first in 36 years, of her history making jaunt to the Sussex coast.

The Brooks auction of Collectors' Motor Cars and Automobilia took place at Olympia 2, Hammersmith Road, London, on Thursday December 2nd 1993 at 6pm. Prior viewing was by appointment from Monday November 15th to Friday November 26th, as well as on auction day itself from 10am up until proceedings began in the evening. Admission was by catalogue only. This beautifully-illustrated booklet of some 96 pages features descriptive detail and supporting illustrations of all 175 lots offered for sale. Saluting the significance of this particular event, the catalogue cover depicts a black and white scene from the film, showing John Gregson and Dinah Sheridan in their respective roles as Alan and Wendy McKim puzzling over a mechanical fault with Genevieve's engine.

The memorabilia collection on offer included such gems as an original 1927 poster for the Miramas Grand Prix de l'ACF; a first edition 1924 driver's handbook belonging to a Sunbeam 20/60hp; *Automobiles of The World* – a rare publication detailing all current manufacturers' models for 1921; a continental silver cigarette

The National Motor Museum, Saturday October 30th 1993. Genevieve with Marjory Cornelius, Lord Montagu of Beaulieu, Larry Adler, and the author.

case in the shape of an early motor car radiator, circa 1912; a very rare early motor town-carriage interior flower holder, in the art nouveau-style, hallmarked and stamped Mappin Bros London 1900; a fine and seldom-seen set of six 1905 sterling silver menu holders, in the shape of veteran cars designed and produced by George and Charles Asprey, and stamped with the maker's mark. There was an early cylinder-type hand-cranked petrol pump from the 1920s; Edwardian motoring goggles; and a prewar leather driving helmet. Lot 63 was a chromolithograph 76 x 102 promotional colour poster advertising the film *Genevieve*, which carried a price expectation of between £500 and £700. Lot 64 also happened to be a rare trophy plaque, showing a *Genevieve* film scene in bas-relief bronze-effect cast plaster, with silver inset on the base and inscribed 'The Genevieve Trophy.' These had been originally presented to the owners of the numerous cars used in the film. This particular example was expected to fetch between £150 and £220.

Lots 145 to 175 were the vehicles being offered, some perhaps more interesting than others. A 1929 4.5-litre Bentley, for example; a 1938 Olympia show stand exhibit in the form of a 2-litre Frazer Nash-BMW 327 convertible cabriolet; a 1952/53 2-litre Formula 2 OSCA Monoposto racing single-seater; a 1981 4.8-litre Ferrari 400i Berlina by Pininfarina; a Mulliner-bodied 1933 3.7-litre Rolls-Royce 20/25 Six Light saloon, originally the property of His Grace The Duke of Somerset; and, of course, lot number 148, the 1904 12hp Darracq known as Genevieve. Chassis no 6505, engine no 6060, which – as the

Continued page 138

Ken Taylor, who restored Genevieve in Western Australia for the late Paul Terry, explains a few points to the author outside Brooks.

Genevieve arrives from Beaulieu at Brooks the auctioneer, Clapham Common West Side, London.

The author waiting for Ken Taylor to get Genevieve ready for a run through Clapham.

catalogue stated – 'with her two-seater bodywork, flared front wings and twinkling brass work, came to epitomise the typical veteran car to the general public who had once seen her image on every type of souvenir.'

Finally, on Thursday December 2nd, veteran car enthusiasts packed into London's Olympia. There they watched and listened with an element of disbelief as they learned that a mere £130,000 was all that it would take to snap up the accepted world-wide mascot of the veteran car movement. The lucky bidders happened to be the privately-owned Dutch National Motor Museum, established by the Louwman family.

Brooks, which merged with the privately owned auction house Bonhams in 2001, did an excellent job in publicising the sale. The fact that far greater prices were being touted as buying codes for Genevieve may have been responsible for lessening interest in possible purchasers, and going some way to explaining the eventual price that was paid. £500,000 had been expected.

Given the hue and outcry over the nature of her departure from the UK all those years before, and the fanfare that trumpeted her return, there is some irony in the fact that it seems no-one was prepared – or indeed felt it financially worthwhile – to keep her there. Holland – the country of

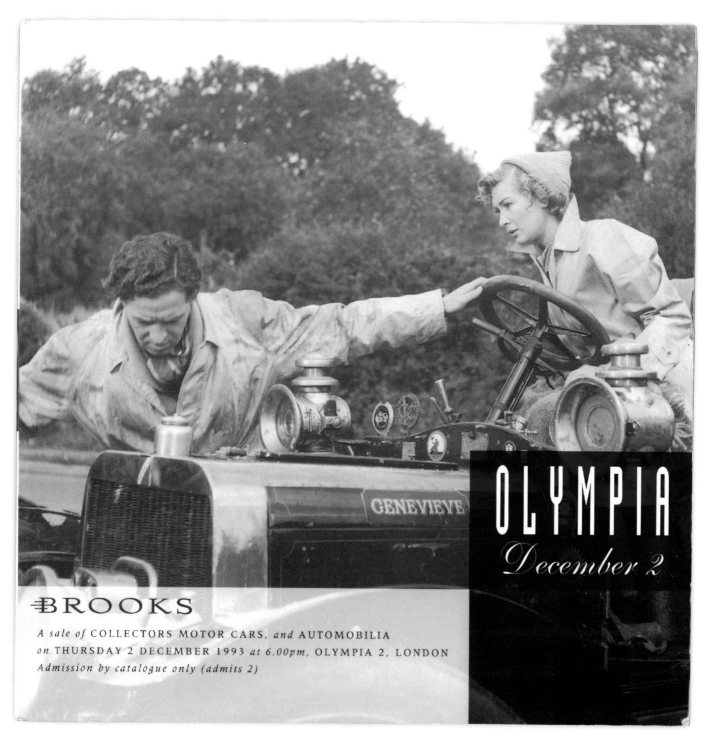

Brooks catalogue cover announcing Genevieve's auction, lot no 148,
Thursday, December 2nd 1993, at 6pm in Olympia 2, London.

STARS: Genevieve, Gregson and Sheridan

Dutch treat at £130,000 for old Genevieve

GENEVIEVE, the world's most famous old car, was sold for £130,000 last week.

The 89-year-old motor caught popular imagination in 1953 as the mechanical star of the classic British film comedy, Genevieve.

Veteran car enthusiasts descended on London's Olympia in droves to join in the bidding. There had been hopes that the price would reach £500,000 — but the French-made 12hp Darracq was bought by the Dutch national motor museum for what looked like a good price.

Genevieve was brought back to England after a 35-year absence in Australia and New Zealand.

The old lady came to fame when producer Henry Cornelius made a film about the London to Brighton rally.

The film starred four of the most popular stars of the time: Kenneth More, John Gregson, Kay Kendall and Dinah Sheridan.

The car was subsequently taken by a private collector to New Zealand and then to Australia. She was sold in 1989 to another collector and, following his recent death, his family returned the car to London for sale.

Her new Dutch owners promised to allow Genevieve to continue competing in the London-Brighton run.

One of many press announcements following Genevieve's sale to the Louwman Motor Museum in Holland.

origin of the Spyker, Genevieve's arch-rival — became home to them both. The sale did have a positive spin-off for veteran motoring enthusiasts; Evert Louwman declared his intention to see Genevieve resume her historic participation in the annual November London to Brighton run for veteran vehicles. This was music to the ears of many, who feared the prospect of the famous car being retired into private museum life. The family continues to be true to its word, recognising as it does the visual impact Genevieve has on her adoring public.

Evert's daughter Quirina underlined this, recalling the first time she joined her father in Genevieve as his passenger in the London to Brighton run. While having long since come to terms with the movie and Genevieve's contribution to the worldwide veteran motoring industry, nothing had really prepared the Louwman family for the nostalgic reaction to seeing the car in person. From the public's obvious fascination in Hyde Park, to seeing her chug along the familiar route to the south coast, recognised and hailed as an old friend by the crowds along the way, it was something of a revelation to the new Dutch owners. "It was a magical experience," recalled Quirina, "especially as Genevieve had not been seen in England for decades. Coming across so many people who shared the same name as our car, and because of it, has been another phenomenon we've had to get used to as well. Just driving the Darracq is an event in itself. When the whistle is sounded people seem to know where it's coming from and call 'Genevieve, look it's Genevieve,' that's so special. She starts

Continued page 143

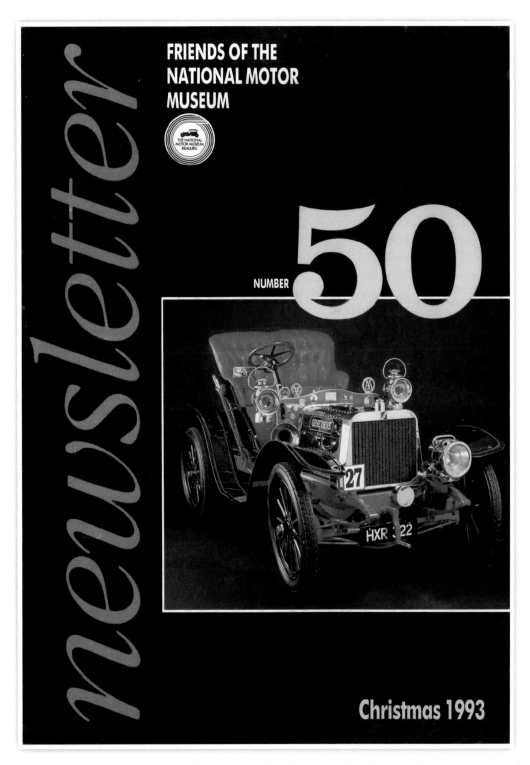

The 1993 Christmas edition of 'The Friends Of The National Motor Museum' journal.

*A promotional Bonhams advert, incorporating Brooks the auctioneer,
seller of veteran, vintage and classic cars.*

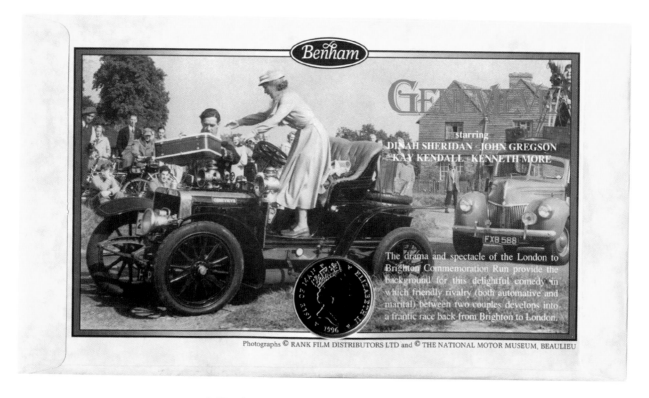

A 'Benham' Genevieve coin cover, 1996.

so beautifully as well and has never let us down, always finishing the Brighton run without fault. Getting down from the car and touching wood is always a good omen for the next outing. The car just seems to make people smile, as it does us. We are always amazed at the people we know, and get to know, who religiously sit down and watch the movie the day before either partaking in or just watching the annual run to Brighton from the roadside."

CHAPTER
SEVENTEEN

In 2001, the Mid Eastern division of the Veteran Car Club of Great Britain hatched a plan to celebrate the 50th anniversary of *Genevieve* going before the cameras in September 1952. This, they decided, would take the form of a weekend rally, retracing the location spots that had become such a highlight of the eventual on-screen production. Getting everything together was quite a task, and took a good year or more to organise. There was no chronological order attached to what the planning committee aimed for, just as there hadn't been 50 years before. Some locations proved more elusive than others, owing to changes attributed to the passage of time, but the success rate of tracking down the essential key settings as well as the more obvious ones was certainly commendable. Genevieve's movie run to Brighton was of course meant to follow the accepted route from London's Hyde Park down to the Sussex coast, a road easily recognised by all familiar with the traditional November jaunt. Filming was well off track in that respect, but then so was the weather. After all, who has ever seen the trees in Hyde Park full and green-leafed in November, as the veterans line up for the 54-mile drive south?

Nonetheless, the elements – and indeed the route depicted in the film – were very much a

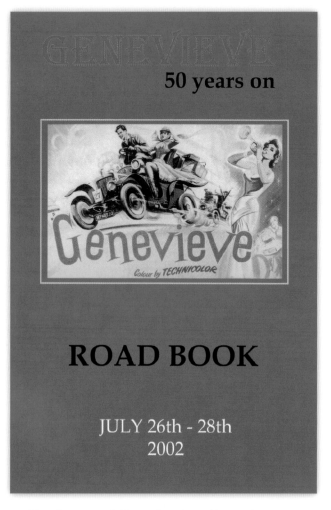

Front cover of Genevieve's 50th anniversary road book, July 2002.

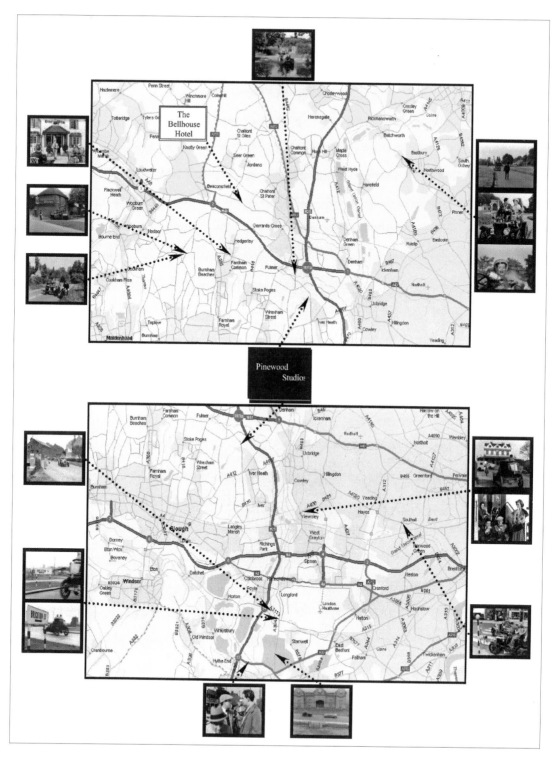

Map in Genevieve's 50th anniversary road book, showing where scenes from the movie were filmed.

Rutland Gate Mews, Knightsbridge, London, where the McKims lived. Revisited during Genevieve's 50th anniversary celebrations (as reproduced in the 2002 Genevieve – 50 Years On road book).

stab in the dark affair, shot mainly in a hotchpotch of locations in and around deepest, darkest Buckinghamshire (albeit within honking distance of Pinewood Studios at Iver Heath). Recognisable, of course, are the Law Courts in the Strand, along with Rutland Gate Mews wedged in-between Knightsbridge's Brompton and Kensington Roads. There were sundry other scenes variously filmed in Hyde Park itself and at the finishing post along Madeira Drive in Brighton, although the latter – because of distance – was not included in the fiftieth anniversary event. Moor Park in Hertfordshire, Southall Broadway, the Embankment, and Westminster Bridge were some settings more readily accessed, and therefore easier to revisit.

Continued page 150

Storyboard and production sketches from the opening Law Court scenes, retraced 50 years later as documented in the 2002 Genevieve – 50 Years On road book.

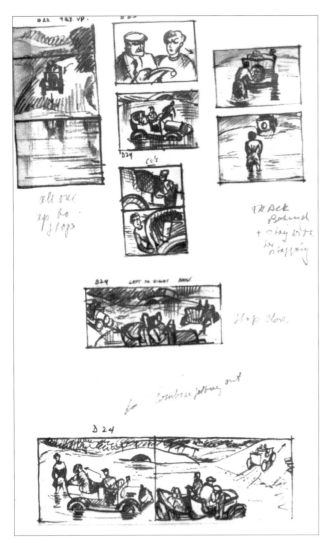

This page & opposite: Where the Spyker got stuck in the ford, Hawkswood Lane, Fulmer, Buckinghamshire; also returned to 50 years later for the anniversary run (as reproduced in the Genevieve – 50 Years On road book).

What eventually came together as the anniversary rally, over the final weekend of July 2002, was an experience never to be forgotten by those taking part. As a permanent record of the occasion, an illustrated road book *Genevieve – 50 Years On* was produced. This brought together, as best as possible, original notes, photos and storyboard illustrations used in making the film, as well as excerpts from the working manuscript owned by Henry Cornelius with photos of the original settings and their equivalents half a century later. A section is devoted to the mood of the characters taking part in the production of the film, and how the actors were required to get into the right frame of mind for each scene.

The souvenir publication, among other things, also visually recorded the rally routes designed to take in film locations, of which there were seven. Each was well researched, detailed, and variously attributed to the main stars Dinah Sheridan, John Gregson, Kay Kendall, Kenneth More, or – in some cases – the names of the characters they played.

The last surviving star of the film cast, Dinah Sheridan, reunited with Genevieve at Pinewood Studios July 2002.

Quirina Louwman, daughter of Genevieve's owner, with Dinah Sheridan in the Darracq at Pinewood.

On the Sunday of that memorable anniversary weekend rally drivers and their cars returned to Pinewood Studios, where the final day's filming of *Genevieve* had taken place in November 1952. Waiting to receive them was the last remaining human star of what has become recognised as one of the British motion picture industry's most successful movies, Dinah Sheridan. There to welcome her back was Genevieve herself, driven by the owner's daughter Quirina Louwman.

For the 82-year-old actress it was an event charged with emotional memories. Her official duties were to present two commemorative plaques, to Genevieve and the Spyker, inscribed with 'British Comedy Society – *Genevieve* 50th anniversary, Dinah Sheridan, Kenneth More, John Gregson, Kay Kendall.' What Dinah didn't know was that she also would be the recipient of a third plaque, identical to the others, a presentation taking her completely by surprise. Surrounded by fascinated rally participants and onlookers, Wendy McKim, for the first time since 1952, climbed back up into the Darracq's passenger seat. Wearing a replica Edwardian driving bonnet, as she had worn in the film, hearts stood still as the past came running back; Dinah, all but overcome, fought off tears for John, Kay, and Kenneth, who were no longer there with her.

Remarkably though, the cars and their star weren't entirely alone. Participating that weekend was Peter Tacon driving his 1903 Humber Forecar, the only owner/driver to recreate his film appearance in Genevieve exactly as he had done 50 years before. This unusual machine was developed from the chain-driven motorcycle by replacing the single front wheel with two, so that a long skirted lady passenger could join the driver. This suited the flat lands of Norfolk, where the vehicle spent the first 84 years of its life, but not in any way practical for the rolling downs of Sussex where the Tacons were to make their home; because there were no gears, the driver had to help it up the hills by slipping the clutch and peddling. When the previous Norfolk owner had no further need for it on the road, he used it to block up a hole in a hedge. Peter Tacon became the new owner for 15 shillings, and set about a full restoration. The Forecar has completed many London to Brighton runs, with a cruising speed of just 24mph, but in 1987 failed to finish due to the clutch coming to pieces; it shed bits over 200yds of road, which were unable to be found afterward. New rollers were subsequently bought, with other bits sawn and filed.

Sadly for all concerned, Marjory Cornelius, the film's costume designer, and widow of the producer/director Henry Cornelius, died suddenly within days of these anniversary celebrations. Hers had been a pivotal role in the weekend's planning process, supplying illustrative contributions and recollections which had been invaluable for the organisers.

Genevieve's participation in the annual London to Brighton run is ongoing. In the main, she can be found at home at the Louwman Dutch National Motor Museum in The Hague. All its exhibits are housed in a magnificent purpose-built establishment, designed by Michael Graves & Associates of Princeton, New Jersey. The building – although modern and opened in July 2010 by Queen Beatrix – reflects elements of traditional Dutch architecture, with steep peaked roof lines complimented by a brick facade set in a special woven pattern. Inside, spread over three exhibition floors, 250 historic cars are displayed, along with motoring artwork and memorabilia accumulated by two generations of the Louwman family. A vision begun in 1934 with the purchase of a 20-year-old Dodge by the present owner's

Commemorative plaque issued to mark Genevieve's 50th anniversary.

Genevieve with the Spyker at the Louwman Museum in Holland, displayed in front of screened images from the film that made her famous.

father, it is now regarded as one of the world's finest collections of its type, and includes some of the most beautiful vehicles ever made.

There are some incredible examples from the earliest years of motoring, such as a totally original 1887 De Dion Bouton et Trepardoux steam quadricycle; an 1894 Peugeot Type 6 Phaeton with Capote; an 1897 Daimler 6hp twin-cylinder six-seater brake; as well as majestic luxury cars of the 1930s, and those that show the first attempts at affordable family motoring. Some are the only examples ever made, whilst others represent extremely limited editions. There are sports and racing cars driven by legendary Grand Prix names, along with Le Mans and those associated with Indianapolis. Other showstoppers include celebrity cars owned by Elvis Presley, Steve McQueen, and Sir Winston Churchill, along with vehicles that have featured in films, such as the taxi from *The Godfather* and the Aston Martin driven by James Bond in *Goldfinger* and *Thunderball.*

Quite obviously, Genevieve is in good company here, particularly as – in her own display area – she can keep an eye on her film adversary, the 1904/05 12/16hp Spyker Double Phaeton, which is parked directly opposite and which has long since forgiven 'that French Darracq' for reaching Westminster Bridge first in the famous on-screen race back to London. Is it any wonder that the Spyker's film appearance prompted, in 1956, the establishment of the Dutch Pionier Automobielen Club; indeed, at the Louwman Museum one can see an extensive display of Dutch-made Spykers, underlining Holland's significant contribution to motoring history. These include the 60hp four wheel drive racing machine of 1903, and the 1922 luxurious Spyker C4 all-weather coupé, upholstered in simulated snake skin.

Frank Reece, who passed away in 1963, left instructions that his cherished bright green Spyker – built at the Trompenberg factory in the Netherlands, which also turned out the Dutch royal family's golden carriage – should be returned to its country of origin. With its Dutch engine and mechanical parts, and its English frame, it was

In their own front yard; a Darracq and a Spyker, at Leidsestraatweg 57, The Hague, Netherlands.

duly purchased by the Dutch Autotron Max Lips Collection at Rosmalen for £3000. During its 30 years at the Autotron theme park, the Spyker underwent a complete rebuild, returned back to its original condition, and was entered in rallies all over the world before finding its present home, once again alongside Genevieve at Louwman's, in 2002.

Given that to participate in the London to Brighton run a car must be no newer than 1904, the subject of not only Genevieve's suitability as much as the Spyker's has often been the subject of conjecture. The Darracq's dating has long ago been accepted as 1904, and not a year later as some back in the 1950s believed to be the case. The Spyker was always thought to be a 1905 vehicle, and by rights a non-starter for the Brighton run. Frank Reece's daughter Elaine points out that following the success of the film, her father's car – although actually built in 1904 – was re-dated by the VCC to 1905, precluding it from further participation in the London to Brighton; a mystifying decision, to say the least.

As the roles that made both the Darracq and the Spyker so noteworthy are screened on the wall behind them at the Louwman Museum, no one watching could be left in any doubt what these two have come to mean to the world of veteran motoring. They appear to smile rather benignly toward each other, and look quite content with their own impact.

"Alan, what are we doing this afternoon?"

"I'm tinkering with Genevieve, she's making strange noises."

"She never makes anything else."

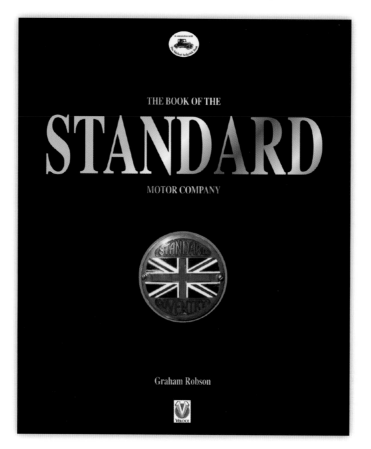

Starting with the original Standard prototype of 1903, this book covers the scores of Standard models built until the brand was discontinued in 1963 (Britain) and 1987 (India). It also covers the Ferguson tractor involvement, military aero-engine manufacture, military aircraft manufacturer (including Beaufighter and Mosquito fighter-bombers), Rolls-Royce Avon turbo-jet military engine manufacture, and Triumph cars.

ISBN: 978-1-845843-43-4
Hardback • 25x20.7cm • £35.00* UK/$69.95* USA • 208 pages • 262 colour and b&w pictures

For more info on Veloce titles, visit our website at www.veloce.co.uk • email: info@veloce.co.uk
• Tel: +44(0)1305 260068 * prices subject to change, p&p extra

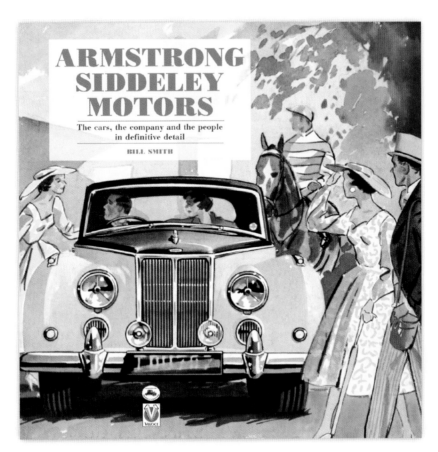

What did Armstrong Siddeley Motors achieve? A car that looked good, did what it was intended to do and was thoroughly reliable. If ever there was a car that exuded style it was the Armstrong Siddeley. From the leviathans of the 1920s to the Art Deco-inspired cars of the thirties, and the restrained post modernism of the 1950s, this is the turbulent story of a great British marque. Nearly 500 pages!

ISBN: 978-1-904788-36-2
Hardback • 25x25cm • £75* UK/$139.95* USA • 496 pages • 365 b&w pictures

For more info on Veloce titles, visit our website at www.veloce.co.uk •
email: info@veloce.co.uk • Tel: +44(0)1305 260068
* prices subject to change, p&p extra

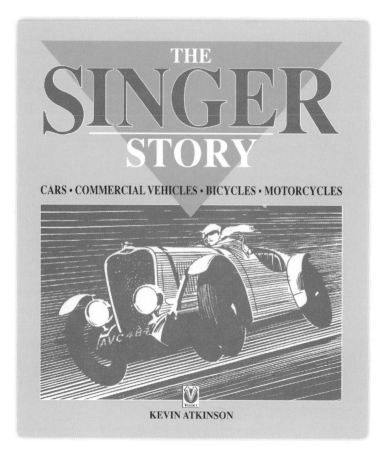

Here is the definitive history of one of Britain's oldest and most important and influential car manufacturers. Thoroughly researched and with over 300 photos this is an important piece of automotive history.

ISBN: 978-1-874105-52-7
Hardback • 25x20.7cm • £60.00* UK/$120* USA • 256 pages • 300+ b&w pictures

For more info on Veloce titles, visit our website at www.veloce.co.uk •
email: info@veloce.co.uk • Tel: +44(0)1305 260068
* prices subject to change, p&p extra

INDEX

a'Court, Robert Holmes 117
Academy Awards, The 67, 68
Adler Larry 7, 64, 67, 68, 96, 132, 135
Airfix 86, 87
Alfa Romeo 11
Allday, G James 87
America's Cup 122
Anderson, Andrew "Andy" 76
Anonima Lombarda Fabbrica Automobili 11
Appointment in London 43
Argyll 15, 16, 127
Aston Martin 153
Aucoc, Jean 9
Australian Modern Motor 88
Autocar, The 10, 13
Automobiles of The World 133

Bailey, Bill 15
Balcon, Michael 33
Barclay-White, Cathy 8
BBC 57
Beaded Wheels 6, 76, 77
Benham 8, 143
Bentley 135
Benz 24, 87
  Dogcart 87
Bloom, Claire 43
Blue Mountains Rally 87, 90
Bluebird 11
Bogarde, Dirk 43, 50
Bond, James 153
Bonhams 8, 138, 142
Brooks 133, 137-9, 142
Bugatti 117
  Royale 117
Buick 106

Cadby, Charlie 24, 26, 27, 42
Cadillac 64, 84, 119
Campbell, Malcom 11
Carr, Susan 130

Challis, Christopher 7, 36
Christchurch Star 112
Churchill, Sir Winston 153
Claverhouse, Ambrose 28, 29, 32, 44, 62, 64
Clegg, Owen 11
Confederation of Australian Motorsport 125
Cornelius, Henry 33, 35, 36, 39, 42-4, 50,
    54, 62, 64, 66-8, 87, 127, 150, 152
Cornelius, Marjory 7, 8, 33, 35, 43, 44, 54,
    62, 87, 132, 135, 152
Coronation Rally 76, 82

Daily Telegraph, The 15, 19
Daimler 16, 17, 127, 153
  Landaulet 17
Darracq, Alexandre 9
De Dion Bouton 24, 42, 61
De Dion Bouton et Trepardoux 153
Decauville 24
Deep Blue Sea, The 44
Disney 64, 107
Dreamworld 107
Durkopp 24
Dutch Jubilee Rally, 1961 98
Dutch Rally, 1954 82

Edwards, Michael 8
Emancipation Run, The 9
Essex Super Six 17

Fairhurst, Henry 24
Farman, Henri 11
Ferrari 135
Flapper 11
Flying Fifteen 14, 21, 24
Ford 17, 21, 22, 24, 42, 93, 122
  Model T 17, 21, 122
Ford, Henry 122
Frazer Nash-BMW 135
Freyberg VC, Lord 80
Galloping Major, The 33

Gatsonides, Maus 82
Genevieve – 50 Years On 8, 146-8, 150
Genevieve 500 8, 122, 125-30
Genevieve 2002 Anniversary Rally 8
Genevieve Foundation 126
Genevieve – The story of the film 83
Gilltrap, George Jnr 8, 107, 115, 117, 118, 122
Gilltrap, George Snr 83, 84, 87, 90, 93, 94,
    96, 101, 103, 105-7, 111
Gilltrap, Kathleen 5, 7, 101, 107, 111
Gilltrap's Auto Museum 95, 96, 107, 115, 117
Gladiator 9, 87
Godfather, The 153
Goldfinger 153
Goodwood 82
Great American Race 125
Gregson, John 2, 5, 6, 8, 28, 38, 39, 42, 44,
    47, 50, 57, 64, 76, 82, 133, 150, 151
Guess Who's Coming to Dinner 28
Gunn, George 36

Hemery, Victor 11
Hooper 119
Hotchkiss 17
Humber 17, 42, 152
  Forecar 152

International Federation of Veteran Car
    Clubs 98, 106
International Rally for Vintage and Veteran
    Cars 5, 98, 103, 107
It Ain't Necessarily So 7
It Always Rains on Sundays 33
It's a Mad, Mad, Mad, Mad World 28

Jeep 84

Keating, John 127
Kendall, Kay 2, 6, 29, 39, 44, 47, 56, 62-4,
    150, 151
Korda, Alexander 33

Lanchester 42
Laredo, Rodney 8, 114, 115, 132, 135, 138
Le *Figaro* 73
Le Mans 153
Le Matin 26
Lemon, Elaine 8, 127, 154
Little Four, The 33
London to Brighton Veteran Car Run 6, 9,
    15, 26, 28, 31, 36, 40, 44, 51, 60, 82,
    87, 125, 130, 133, 140, 143, 152, 154
London Town 44
Louwman, Evert 140
Louwman Motor Museum 8, 140, 153, 154
Louwman, Quirina 140, 151

Marx, Groucho 35
Matchbox 84
Mathieson, Muir 67, 68
McKim, Alan 5, 9, 28-32, 43, 44, 57, 61, 64,
    133, 154
McKim, Wendy 5, 9, 28-32, 43, 44, 57, 61,
    64, 133, 151
McQueen, Steve 153
Mercedes 17
Millet 9
Miramas Grand Prix de l'ACF 133
Mitchell, Leslie 57
Montagu, Lord 106, 112, 132, 133, 135
Monte Carlo Rally 82
More, Kenneth 2, 6, 28, 39, 44, 47, 57, 62,
    64, 127, 150, 151
Morris 17
Motor Sport 8, 19, 22, 24
Mulliner 135

Nagle, Elizabeth 106, 133
National Film Finance Corporation 33
National Motor Museum, Netherlands 138,
    152
National Motor Museum, UK 7, 106, 112, 115,
    117, 130, 132, 133, 135, 137, 141, 152

Oldsmobile 42
OSCA 135

Passport to Pimlico 33
Pau Auto Race 11
Paul Terry Organisation 8
Peacock, Bill 7, 15, 17-9, 21, 24, 127
Peters, Rosalind 29, 62
Peugeot 153
    Type 6 Phaeton 153
Picturegoer 74
Pinewood Studios 33, 42, 51, 64, 73, 146,
    150, 151
Presley, Elvis 153

Railway Children, The 6
Rank, J Arthur 28, 60
Rank Organisation 28, 33, 36, 39, 40, 64,
    67, 68, 73, 80, 132
Rattigan, Terrance 44
Reece brothers, The 19
Reece, Frank 8, 16, 43, 78, 127, 153, 154
Reeves, Albert 24
Reeves, Norman 6, 7, 19, 22, 24, 26, 27, 42,
    76-8, 82, 87, 93, 94, 107, 122
Renault 8/10 15
Rolls-Royce 119
Rootes 83, 84
Rose, Tania 7, 33, 133
Rose, William 7, 24, 28, 32, 34-36, 42, 56,
    58, 133

Sheridan, Dinah 2, 5-7, 28, 37-39, 43, 44,
    47, 50, 51, 56, 67, 127, 130, 133,
    150-152
Silverstone 82
Smith, Sir Henry Abel 96, 98
Socrates 19
Southward, Len 106
Spyker 8, 16, 19, 28, 37, 42-4, 47, 57, 62, 78,
    84, 127, 140, 148, 151, 153, 154
    C4 153

Double Phaeton 153
St John, Earl 33, 39
Stanley Steamer 84
STD Motors 11
Sunbeam 11, 15, 16, 19, 133
Suzie the Dog 56, 62
Sydney Morning Herald, The 8, 90

Talbot 11
Taylor, Ken 122, 133, 137, 138
Technicolor 7, 36, 39, 127
Terry, Paul 8, 112, 117-9, 122, 123, 125, 126,
    128, 130, 133, 137
Thornycroft 16
Thunderball 153
Turner, Rex 87, 90
TVW7 Perth 8

United Artists 67

Vauxhall 106
    Prince Henry 106
Venning, Peter 7, 18, 19, 21, 22, 26
Veteran Car Club of Australia 122
Veteran Car Club of Great Britain 28, 40,
    57, 68, 73, 84, 122, 127, 132, 144,
    154
Veteran Car Gazette 68
Vintage Car Club of New Zealand 6, 76,
    77
Voiturette 11

Wadsworth, Jack 15, 17-9
West Australian, The 8
Where No Vultures Fly 43
White, James Dillon 83
Whitlock Aster 16
Whyte, Colin 114
Withers 16
Wolseley 42
World War One 15, 17, 130
World War Two 18, 43, 83